A FATHER'S LOVE?

Felicity Allen

ARCHWAY
PUBLISHING

Archway Publishing books may be ordered through booksellers or by contacting:

Archway Publishing
1663 Liberty Drive
Bloomington, IN 47403
www.archwaypublishing.com
844-669-3957

ISBN: 978-1-6657-2859-1 (sc)
ISBN: 978-1-6657-2858-4 (hc)
ISBN: 978-1-6657-2860-7 (e)

Library of Congress Control Number: 2022914970

Print information available on the last page.

Archway Publishing rev. date: 10/12/2022

We have to support survivors and help break the silence. We need to make the invisible visible. It's time to change the things we cannot accept.

—Daniela Ligiero,
CEO of Together for Girls

Dedication

To my husband, my son, and my daughter. Without the love you have shown me in my life, I am not sure I would've become the person I am today. Thank you. I love you all so much.

ONE

My name is Felicity, and I am thirty years old. I'm currently lying in my bed with my four dogs in our yurt tent, which just so happens to be on my mother and stepfather's property. My husband and I had sold our house in New York and decided to move our family to North Carolina. We were pretty young when we purchased our house—my husband was twenty-five and I was twenty-two. It was a great opportunity, not a lot of couples are able to say they've reached a milestone like that at that age, but maybe we moved a little too fast. Or maybe we had grown and were in search of new desires.

Therefore, we packed everyone and everything up in hopes of a better opportunity at this thing called life—our two children, four dogs, two cats, and a ferret, all ready to start anew. We were hoping to start fresh while learning from mistakes we'd made when we were younger—mistakes when it came to finances and credit, poor decisions, and short-term thinking. Maybe we'd get peace of mind, moving from a city of about a quarter million to the countryside, which had a population of about eight thousand. Listening to the leaves fall this morning, I am happy to have gotten away to focus on my family and myself.

I can honestly say that I love and adore my family. I say the word "honestly" because the words "marriage," "family," and "love" all seemed to have lost their meaning over the years. My husband and I have been together for quite some time now, a little over a decade, and we have two amazing children. They bicker and argue like kids typically do with their siblings, but they love each other unconditionally. They're always the first ones to stick up for each other; I couldn't wish for better children. I couldn't ask for a better husband either. He makes me feel so good when I'm feeling low, and he makes me feel great when I'm feeling good. He always makes me feel truly loved. My kids are the same—true cuddle bugs. Always wanting love and affection and always giving it. They even argue about who makes a better egg sandwich for me in the morning. I can truly say I'm incredibly honored to have a family like the one I have now.

I always say that we are your typical family. We work and our kids go to school; they have extracurricular activities they are involved in. I work full-time, and ever since COVID-19 plagued our world and changed our lives, I've been able to work from home. The company I work for is amazing. The days are mentally hard and long, but the people are awesome—very family oriented—and my boss is probably the best boss I've ever had. No, I lied. My boss is definitely the best boss I've ever had. He even puts up with my sassy attitude and sometimes foul language. My husband renovates and remodels homes, and has recently started his own business.

Due to COVID-19 creating an uncertain future in the education system, the kids actually started their first year of homeschooling this year, and they love it. My son wanted to learn French, which he's really excited about, and my daughter chose Spanish. Both of the kids stay pretty busy as well with jiu-jitsu, Muay Thai, cheerleading, and Girl Scouts, but they love it and even get upset when we have to miss a day. Like I said, your typical family. Our kids bicker sometimes, but no more than any other siblings, and they love each other so much that they try to do the other's chores when one is sick. My husband and I hardly ever argue, if at all. He's so laid back and calm. I am the one who's quite rowdy. He's definitely the yin to my yang—my better half, as the saying goes.

I can't help but sometimes feel like I'm a fraud though. I think to myself, *How are you happy?* With the things I've gone through in my life, how am I happy? I mean, I'm grateful and thankful that I am able to have the life that I have, but I see people who have gone through similar things that have turned out so awful. They're sad or depressed, lost, or just completely broken from the traumatizing events they have gone through. Like I said, I'm thankful I didn't end up like that. I'm happy and have a healthy family with healthy relationships.

I see people who go through trauma and then turn to God, which seems to help them. I still find it hard to believe in God. I get emotional when I go to church and when I listen to the choir, but to say I am a believer would be a lie. I used to get asked if I believe in God a lot, actually. I usually wanted to say no, and sometimes I did, but when people ask why, how do you just come out and say, "Because I was molested half of my life, and I don't believe that there would be a god who'd allow that kind of thing to happen." So I just say, "I don't know—haven't seen enough proof yet."

Deciding to write this book didn't come easily either. I have racked my brain for years about whether or not I should write this autobiography. There are a lot of factors that came into my decision, like how would it affect my kids? What would my husband think of me? Would he be disgusted? Could this affect my job or my relationships with my friends? What will happen to him, my dad?

Do you ever get that feeling in your chest? The feeling that you need to say something. Then your chest gets really heavy and you never say it. Afterward, it feels like a brick is weighing on your chest. That's how I feel most of the time. If you ask anybody who knows me, they would say that I usually don't shy away from saying something that's on my mind. This is hard, but I feel like writing this will get this weight off my chest. I know it might sound selfish, and I know it might hurt people in the process. However, I think it's about time I start looking after myself. I need to stop worrying about those who hurt me, those who took my innocence.

I wish I could be a hundred percent honest and say I am all for writing this book and letting all of you in on my life, but that would be a lie. Even now, I'm so torn about writing the rest of this book. There's a fine line, I believe, when writing about molestation between anyone. I mean, you want to be informative and descriptive, but you also want to make sure what you're writing isn't getting the next pedophile off just by reading your book. It's a sickening thought to be honest, but I can't help but think about it. I want to be a hundred percent transparent in writing this though. I hope this can help others who have gone through something similar. I'm going to be writing about things I've never spoken out loud to anyone about, not even to my husband. Most of what I'm going to tell you has been locked away in that brick on my chest.

Now I will say this: I don't blame all of my hardships and bad memories for any unhappiness or problems that I have now as an adult. I think I give my hardships and bad memories more credit for making me who I am; for helping me become who I am now. That's all you can do, right? You can't change the past. I do think about my childhood often though. I think about how it was all messed up. I always say that it could have been worse, and I can't help but feel like I shouldn't think that way. I mean, I did grow up with my mother, father, sister, and brother. My dad was in the military, well-liked by everyone. A real charmer, most people would say. My mom was a stay-at-home mom. My sister and I got along for the most part. And then there was my brother, who hated me.

We lived in California. We lived away from a lot of people and only had a couple of neighbors. From an outsider's perspective, my dad was a great, hardworking, stand-up guy. My mother was beautiful, fun, and always the life of the party. From the outside looking in, we were a good family. Little did they know that the piece-of-shit father liked to touch his daughters while they slept. But he acted like a normal dad in the day. He was great at manipulating the way people thought of him. I had a mother who was depressed and only thought of herself, a sister who stayed to herself, and a brother who hated me for being everything he wasn't, as he would say. I know all families have their issues, and I know all families aren't perfect, but I would have settled for that imperfect normal family over what we had any day.

TWO

I am the youngest of four. My oldest brother was from my dad's first wife. My second oldest brother and older sister shared the same mother and father that I did. My oldest brother lived with his mom, and we only saw him maybe once a year. I thought we got along just fine until we got older and grew apart. Now he thinks I'm a bitch, and I think he's an asshole; that's pretty much the extent of our relationship. I did reach out to him once to try to get my nieces and nephews gifts for Christmas, but he messaged me back to say, "So are we going to act like we like each other now?" I gave up trying that.

My second oldest brother was born with certain conditions that proved to have life-long effects. He hated his life then—hell, he hates his life now. He and I used to get into the worst arguments. Granted, I was pretty young and probably egged him on a little bit more than I should have. Damn, did he hate me. There was this one time my Rottweiler, Bruno, was lying against the outhouse that we had for the washer and dryer. My brother and his friend were on the roof, and his friend held his hands so my brother could bend over and take a shit on my dog while he slept. Yeah, that was my brother.

He used to get mad at me and say, "It's not fair. Not fair that you're pretty and everyone likes you."

Often our arguments would get so bad he would chase me with a knife. My sister would have to jump in the middle of us, holding him, screaming, "Felicity run!" and I would run into my room and lock the door. Sometimes, I would be in there for a few hours until he calmed down. He would even go to the extent of going outside, picking up dog shit, and throwing it at my window and laughing.

Even though he hated me, I have always stuck up for him. He used to get in so many fights, either standing up for himself against bullies or starting the fight. Either way, I always stuck up for him. I even got in a few fights sticking up for him. There was this guy that always picked on my brother. One night I heard all the neighborhood kids cheering and shouting. I ran over and saw that guy and my brother fighting. The other guy was much bigger than my brother. He got my brother on the ground and started kicking him in his back. I went over there and jumped on the guy. I started yelling and hitting him. The fight finally ended, and when that guy came to our house I went up to him and slapped him right across his face. I told him if he ever did that to my brother again, I would kill him. He just kept apologizing over and over. Then he left.

It didn't matter to my brother then, though, and it doesn't matter now. He truly hated me then, and he still does. Only difference is I was scared of him back then. I'm not anymore, not even a little bit. We don't have much of a relationship to this day.

He had a falling-out with his wife and she took my niece from him and got back with her ex. My brother ended up staying with me for a couple of years. I tried to help him get on the right track in life, but he just never wanted to listen to anything I said. He used to say, "I want what you have—a loving family, nice house, good job, friends!" But he never wanted to put in the time or effort it takes to achieve all of that. He acted as if all of that came to me for free. He never could understand the concept of working hard. Even with his handicaps, he has so many strong talents, but he never had anyone to push him in the right direction. I got him to practice relentlessly until he finally received his permit driving license. I bought him the tools and supplies he needed to start his business for fixing phone screens. I took him to his lawyer and to all his one hour visits with his daughter until he finally got custody of her. I helped take care of his daughter, my niece, but none of that was good enough.

I feel like if he'd had different parents that were there for him from the beginning and had stuck by him, he would be in a much better place in his life. All he needed was a little guidance, but he never got that. He is really good with technology. He can take a game system or computer apart and put it back together. He has talents that could've helped him be successful in his life now; if only he'd had parents that wanted to help him achieve that.

My sister and I were typical sisters growing up. We bickered sometimes, but also had good conversations and laughs that still stick with me to this day. We would joke about the dumbest stuff; but it didn't matter how dumb it was, we still laughed so hard. Other than that, we weren't very close. We were more like distant cousins back then. We didn't go to each other when we had things to talk about, whether it was about Dad or not. We didn't even talk about school or friends—nothing. We talked about jokes or shows. We didn't talk about the important things, though, not until we were a little older. Now that I'm an adult I see that she was trying to protect me in the only way she knew how.

She lives in California with her husband and three kids. She seems happy, which makes me happy. She is a really good mom as well. Sometimes I wonder how she would have ended up if Dad hadn't done what he did to us. I feel like her and I went on separate paths that led to the same ending, if that makes any sense. We are both happy with our families and our lives now, even though our journeys were very different. We're really close now. I've gotten through a lot of bad thoughts and memories with her by my side. I just wish she would stop feeling guilty— to stop feeling guilty for what our dad chose to do. I hope she knows it was no one's fault but his. I hope my writing this book clears the air and helps her as well. She still has insecurities and demons she fights all the time. She's strong though, and I'm here to help her get through anything, always!

THREE

My mom was beautiful, and most of the time she was having fun in some type of way. I honestly don't remember a lot of the beginning years with my mom. I don't know if that's because I was just too young, or if the traumatizing events with my dad overshadowed the good ones with her. One positive thing I do remember is getting toe cramps in my sleep that were so bad they would wake me up, and I would be crying in pain. I would run to her, and she would rub my toes and feet until the cramps were gone. She would talk to me sweetly and calm me down.

She was an artist and sometimes would do painting and arts-and-crafts activities with us. Mom would take us to her friend's house, and they would have parties. A bunch of adults would go, and they would bring their kids. So all the adults would be inside drinking, listening to music, and the kids would be outside playing manhunt or other games of that nature.

I remember times she would walk us down that long dirt road, often to the bus stop. I even have memories of driving in her purple Cadillac really fast down the dirt road over the bumps. As a young child, I found that exciting and exhilarating. As much as I remember the fun stuff, I remember the not so fun things as well; such as seeing her cry all of the time. Her and Dad were always screaming at each other, while we were in our rooms with the door shut, crying. How she never let us decorate for Christmas. We would come home from school and it would all be done. We could only hang up a couple of ornaments on the tree, and even then she would move them.

I also remember how often she would sleep all day and night. Dad coming home yelling at her, telling her how lazy she was. I couldn't see it back then, as a child, but now, as an adult, I can see that was a major sign of depression and problems in their relationship. This would eventually come to light. Even the times that she would just leave and none of us knew where she went. Yup, that was my relationship with my mom.

My dad, on the other hand, was different. He worked a lot, that's for sure. He wasn't home a lot then, but when he was home, he would swim with us; he would take us on a ride in the Jeep down the dirt road, going really fast while our dog Coco ran beside the car trying to keep up. I was like his little helper, always the first one to say I wanted to help; always the first one to say, "Dad, let me come help you," even though it was just helping with chores or running errands in town.

My mom and dad would have parties at our house. Their friends, mostly other military friends and some kids, would all come to our house. They would all be smoking their cigarettes, drinking whiskey or beer, and playing poker all night long. I would get everyone's drinks and rub their shoulders when they were getting stressed out about a bad hand, and they would all give me a dollar. I was happy making the five or six bucks during their parties. Just like most families, there were good times and there were bad times. The good times were really good, and the bad times proved to be nightmares that would last a lifetime.

My mother was sometimes there and sometimes not, both mentally and physically. My dad, when I was awake, was an OK dad. When I was asleep, he was the monster that haunted my dreams. He was the demon that took a piece of my soul every night he came into my room.

I grew up sharing a room with my sister. We had separate beds on separate ends of the room. I was just a little girl, in maybe kindergarten or first grade, when I first remember waking up to him. I was waking up but still unable to open my eyes. It was like my mind was awake but my body wasn't. I felt wetness on my toes, and after a few seconds, even though it felt like an eternity, I smelled it. I remember the fragrance that still haunts me to this day. A combination of Irish Spring soap and cigarettes. That was when I realized it was my dad sucking on my toes while I was in my bed. I was sleeping but awake at the same time.

I was so scared I didn't even know what to think, what to do; then I felt like I could move. So I slowly started moving. He jumped up, ran around the front of my bed, tucked me in a little bit, kissed my forehead, and said, "It's OK, sweetheart, I was just tucking you in," right before leaving my room. That was the first time I'd woken up. It scares me to think what may or may not have happened prior to that, things that I just didn't wake up to. That is the very first memory I have of my dad molesting me. Little did I know at that time that things would get worse—so much worse.

I woke up the next morning and saw my sister writing in her diary. She wasn't acting weird or acting like anything had happened. I went into the living room; both of my parents were there, and they seemed normal too, like nothing had happened the night before. I looked out of our living room window and saw my brother outside playing basketball. So there I was, this little girl, confused and scared, with everyone around me acting like absolutely nothing was wrong. I even started thinking to myself that maybe it was all a dream. Maybe I was the one who was fucked up for even imagining that. I was honestly hoping it was just a dream.

I took a shower that night and cried alone while my mind traveled in a million different directions. As a child, I was terrified. I didn't know what to think. I felt alone, like I had nobody to talk to. I couldn't help but think, *Is this my fault? Did I do something to deserve it? Is it normal?* I look back and think about these memories all the time. I wish I could go back to younger me and just be there for myself. Be there to tell myself "It's not your fault; tell someone. You're not alone."

Before that, I was always the first one to want to help my dad with everything. But after that night, everything changed. I didn't want to help him as much—I didn't want to be around him—but he still made me. All I wanted was to create distance between the two of us.

One time, we took a road trip. He had to go help one of his friends in another state. I remember my brother begged to go with him, and my dad said, "No your sister is coming." He made me go with him. Mom didn't say anything, so my brother just pouted, and my sister never wanted to go anywhere with my dad anyway. My dad made Chex Mix, put it in a big bowl, packed us some drinks, and we left.

I was little and I should have been in the back seat, but he made me sit up front. He said it was OK, that he needed my help to stay awake and to pass him snacks. In the beginning of the road trip, I actually had a good time. We were laughing, joking, and singing along to the country music he loved to play so much. It was actually really good for us.

Then I started getting tired, and I was terrified. I didn't want to go to sleep. I remember him looking at me and saying, "Put your legs up, sweetheart, so you could stretch and sleep good."

I said, "No, I'm not tired," and he replied, "Yes you are, Felicity, you were falling asleep. Come on, don't make me tell you again. Put your legs on my lap and take a nap."

I was terrified, but I couldn't say no. How could I? So I put my legs on his lap. I fell asleep and then it happened again. I felt my foot in his hand and his tongue on my toes. I was able to make a grunting noise like I was waking up, and he stopped. He tried to shush me and tell me to go back to sleep, but I said, "No, I'm fine. I'm awake." I put my legs back down on the floor of the car, but I ended up falling asleep again.

The next thing I remember, the car was stopped and it was dark. Once again, my mind woke up before my body, and his tongue was in my mouth this time. It smelled like cigarettes. I couldn't move. I was paralyzed, screaming internally, *Please stop! Please stop! Please stop!* And right before I was able to move he said, "I know you're awake."

My heart felt like it stopped instantly. It was probably the most terrifying moment of my life. The way he said it sent shivers down my spine—like creepy, scary, and disgusting all in one feeling. I waited a minute, then slowly moved. I opened my eyes, waking up fully, and he acted as if nothing had happened, as if he hadn't just done what he did, or even said what he'd said. He was back to normal dad—daytime dad.

FOUR

Growing up, I had some great teachers. I don't remember all of their names, but I do remember little things that they did that made me feel comfortable and happy. I had heard of this one teacher who was an Irishman and over six feet tall. Every year for St. Patrick's Day he would tell his class about leprechauns, and the entire class would set up a trap to catch one. Then the year came that I was finally in his class! Our class made the trap, and then we went to recess and came back to see this trap all messed up—little tiny footprints in the powder of flour or sugar that we'd used. He was so surprised, like, oh-my-gosh guys we almost caught him. He used to bring his wife in, and she always brought desserts, candy, and gifts for the class. I remember I used to think about what it would be like to be their kid; they seemed so happy.

I had another teacher that was in a motorized wheelchair. She would let me help her with all types of things, like passing out papers, or collecting things from the class. It even got to the point where she would pay me to go grocery shopping for her. I was little, but my dad allowed it. She drove to the grocery store, and gave me a list of groceries and an envelope with money. I would go into the grocery store by myself, and it gave me the feeling that I was so big. I would get everything on the list, come out, put all of her stuff in her car, drive with her to her house, and bring it into her kitchen. She would pay me ten, sometimes twenty, dollars, and then she would drive me home.

Another teacher that I had was motherly, fun, and vibrant. I remember how proud she was that her father and she had walked with Martin Luther King Jr. She had a picture of her as a little girl holding his hand and holding her father's hand on her other side. She would tell us stories of countries she'd visited and all of the different things she'd seen. She would show us pictures of these beautiful places and sculptures.

That teacher always made me feel big, like I could do anything in the world that I wanted to. We used to have these conversations after class, and I remember this one time she told me, "Just because you share the same blood with someone doesn't make them your family." She told me I could tell her anything, and if I ever needed her to let her know. I never told her. I wish I had.

I have had my share of amazing teachers, but there are always good and bad teachers, just like there are good and bad people. I had this one teacher that was a really nice lady, a little strict but never mean. She and I never bonded on a deep level, but as far as a teacher-student relationship goes, she was good.

Her husband worked at the school part-time. He wasn't a teacher though; he helped sometimes with the crosswalk. He would come into her class, pass out candy, and be all sweet and nice. He would call me over, and I would go over to him. He would pick me up and put me on his lap. His hand would land right on my butt. I would try to get up, and he would laugh and say something like, "Oh, you don't want another piece of candy?" or "You don't have to go back to work yet, I'm the boss of your teacher."

I remember thinking while I was on his lap, does his wife know that he's making me feel uncomfortable? Does she care? I thought about telling her how he was making me feel. How his hand always landed on my butt.

The last day of school I was wearing a dress and he came in. He called me over and put me on his lap again, asking, "What do you like to do for fun?" My dress was pulled up, and I tried pulling it down. He pulled the dress from underneath my bottom so that the dress was draped over his knee and my panties were on his leg. I went to get up, and he grabbed my arm and said, "Is this really how you want to leave me on the last day of school after all the candy I gave you?"

I just sat there on his knee, trying to think of how I could get up, but then I felt his penis against my leg, like something poking me. I looked at his face, and I could tell he knew what he was doing. I jumped up, ran to the bathroom, and cried. I stayed there the whole recess crying.

I was so angry with myself. I hit myself in the head and face; I pinched my leg until it turned purple. Why couldn't I just say something? Why was I so scared and silent? I wish I'd had the guts back then that I have now. At that point it had already been a couple of years of my dad coming in and out of my room a few days every week, and then this happened with this teacher's husband. I was so confused. *Why is this happening? Is it happening to everyone else? Did I say something to make him think I wanted this? Did I do something to make him think it was OK? What is wrong with me?*

FIVE

The very first memory I have of my dad coming into my room was when he was sucking on my toes. Over the years, that slowly progressed. He started to touch me all over with his hands, touching me in my private areas. My dad then started making me touch him. I woke up with my hand on his penis, and my hand was wet. At the time, I was a little girl and had no idea why it was wet, but as an adult I do. He started lying in bed with me and kind of humping me with my clothes half way off. It just seemed to be getting worse and worse.

I hated going to sleep. I would try so hard to stay awake. My mother was sleeping in the bed next to him every night. My sister was sleeping in the bed on the other side of my room. My brother was sleeping in his bed across from my room. I would think, *Does my mom know? Does she care?* I'd look at my sister and think, *Is he doing it to her too?* I couldn't understand how my dad could leave his bed every night and come to my room, which was on the opposite side of the wall from my parents' room, and yet my mom never knew what was going on. She never knew her husband was leaving almost every night to go to their daughters' room and molest them;

or maybe she did know and she was scared too. I honestly don't think I will ever get the full truth.

I tried my best not to fall asleep. I stayed up for twenty-eight hours once with my friends to see if I could do it at home, but no matter what I tried, I would always end up falling asleep and wake to him invading my room and my body.

It happened almost every night. He would always get mad when I tried to stay the night at a friend's house or the neighbor's house. He would try to make it like I didn't want to be home, or try to make me feel bad. I remember asking myself the same questions as I did with the teacher's husband: *How can he be this way? How can he do this to me? Why is he doing this to me? Is something wrong with me? Did I say something to make him think I wanted this?* As an adult, I realized there's nothing I could say or do that would have stopped this from happening. He was sick and he needed help, but as a child I blamed myself. I always blamed myself.

There's always been two sides to my dad. There was the sober, quiet, and careful one that would tuck me in as he would say goodnight and give me a kiss on the forehead. Then there was the drunk one. The one who would come into my room in his underwear, and as soon as he noticed I was waking up, he would run back to his room like the coward that he was.

Every time drunk dad would leave, I was left with my pants and panties at my ankles. It was so degrading and horrid. I felt like trash. I was just there for him to use and abuse. Being that seven-year-old girl who woke up to my father's fingers in my vagina or in my mouth, or his penis on my lips, prying them open for him to push himself in me. I felt like nothing. Like a blip in reality. I wished so much to wake up before, to try and stop it from happening. But that hardly ever happened.

To this day, I don't understand why I never woke up in the beginning, before he even touched me. Part of me thinks he drugged me. I would always wake up when he was already doing something. Sometimes before my body could react and move, my sister was actually the one that would move or slightly cough, and it would scare him off. He'd run back to his room. I didn't realize what she was doing until I got older. She was trying to help me. She would see him by my bed, and she would start acting like she was waking up so he would leave me alone.

Everything got worse when my mom left. My dad was at work. Mom took us over to her friend's house. She had each of us come out one by one on the porch to talk to us. She cried and hugged me, saying she loved me but she had to go, that she was depressed. She said she would always be there for us as she hugged me. It would be a long time before we hugged again.

After our goodbyes, Dad came in the Pathfinder to pick all three of us up. He said, "Your mother is moving to New York." I don't remember if he said anything else or not, to be honest.

I cried so much in the shower that night. There I was, sitting down in the bathtub as the water hit me. I was shaking. I was so scared. *What's going to happen now? Why does this have to happen? Why does my dad have to be this way? Why can't he be like the day dad he is and not the scary night monster he is?* I saw my dad crying that night in his room reading a note. I remember feeling so bad. I loved my dad, daytime dad anyway. I loved him. He was my dad, after all.

When I was awake during the day, he was actually kind. He would joke and laugh, swim with us, take us places. Well, as many places as he could afford. He was like night and day—the daytime dad made it hard for me to hate the nighttime dad. I was terrified of the nighttime dad, but I didn't hate him. I wanted to hate him, but I couldn't. Honestly, I still don't hate him. I think he's sick. Sick in the mind. I wish he would get the help he needs.

SIX

After my mom left, it got really bad for my brother. My dad hated him. My brother had complications during his delivery. It caused some mental damage, and he didn't talk until he was about five or six years old. He also had some physical handicaps as well, and back then the surgery and recovery was extremely tough.

He used to get picked on a lot, and my dad never cared. It was almost like he was disappointed he didn't have a son that was popular and good in sports or a son that exceled in school. He could have had that with my oldest brother, but he was raised by his mom in another state. You could tell my dad was disappointed; no matter what my brother did, my dad could not be pleased, and that affected my brother in major ways—still does to this day. All he ever wanted was to make my dad proud, and he tried so hard. He still does, even knowing the type of monster my dad is; he still cares about his acceptance. To be honest, I can't even blame him. After everything my dad did to me, I still don't fully hate him, so why should my brother. I have told my brother multiple times that we will never get acceptance, not from him. I have told him that he needs to stop living his life like that, trying to be what he thinks is Dad's perfect image.

My dad was really hard on my sister as well; he always made fun of her and said she was in her own world while calling her ditsy. He made fun of all her friends too. He never acted like he cared about her or about my brother. They weren't close at all, at least not that I can remember. My sister grew to hate him.

My dad cared so much about image and what people thought of us, but he didn't even try to help build up our confidence in any way, shape, or form. It was probably because he was trying to protect his own image, and wanted to paint this picture of a perfect family so that he could deceive people and lead them away from the truth; away from knowing he was the sick pedophile that he was. He would just tear us down; he would make fun of us if we lost weight, make fun of us if we gained weight—it was always a lose-lose situation with him.

Me, on the other hand, I was always his favorite, as sick as that sounds. However, it was true. He wanted me to go everywhere with him, be outside with him, do chores with him, ride my bike while he ran, go swimming together. Now that I'm older, I see what he was doing, but when I was younger, he was all I had. I believe he wanted to spend as much time with me as possible to not only protect his image as a kind and caring father who did everything with his daughter, but also to keep me from other people and limit the possibility of me speaking up.

Daytime dad made sure he was loving to me. He would even tell me how proud he was when I did something good. I don't know if all child molesters are like that—you know, being friends with you, loving you, and then changing and doing awful things to you. We didn't have any family close to where we lived, all we had were neighbors and some friends of the family. It really was just my dad;

he was our main support, and he made sure to use that to his full advantage.

As soon as my mom left, my brother started behaving worse than ever. We used to always go swimming over at the neighbors' house. They had a huge pool equipped with games, a diving board, and a slide. We had a lot of fun there, and their mom was so loving to us.

I was over there swimming one day with our neighbor friends, and my brother runs in and he says, "Oh my God, guys, look what I found. You're never going to believe it." He then sits down by the pool, and he has my sister's diary in his hand. He begins reading it, and it's a memory my sister had of my dad touching her while she was sleeping. My brother tells everyone he can't believe how sick she is, saying this about Dad, how disgusting.

Then she comes over and sees my brother with her diary and instantly starts crying. She goes to him, grabs her diary, and says, "How dare you. This is mine." And he starts bad mouthing and downplaying what she wrote in it about Dad.

I get out of the pool and I say, "It was a dream she had about Dad. It's not real."

I was so embarrassed, and if I felt embarrassed, I know my sister felt a hundred times worse. She ran out crying and I didn't go after her. I have to say, that was one of my biggest regrets, not going after her to console her, to tell her I know, I know what you're going through.

When I heard him say those words in her diary, that's when I knew. I knew Dad was doing it to her too. I never spoke to her about it; part of me believes we had this unspoken bond, almost as if she knew I knew and I knew she knew. So we never needed to talk about it. I feel like we were both too embarrassed to actually come out and say what happened anyways, to actually say the words.

I hated my brother for doing that. He has done a lot of messed up things to us, but that was an all-time low. Obviously I knew he had disabilities, but damn did I hate him after that. All the abuse that my brother put me through—chasing me with knives, throwing poop at my window—nothing pushed me over the edge like that day. I didn't hate him purposely, but to embarrass my sister in front of all of our friends like that … I was disgusted that he was my brother. But the thing that made it worse was how he reacted to her words. I knew the truth and I believed her, but his reaction made me feel like if we ever did speak up, no one would believe us anyways.

Over time it got really bad with my brother, so much so that my dad ended up sending him to my mom. I guess my dad still had a way to contact her over the years. When I got older, she told me that she used to call all the time, but he wouldn't let her speak to us. I don't know how true that is though, since we were left home alone a lot too, and I never got a call from her. It's hard to believe either one of them.

My brother used to call those 1-900 numbers, the ones you would see on late-night television telling you to "call now and speak to the woman of your dreams." He once ran our phone bill up to nearly two thousand dollars. My brother stole from the neighbor, stole her watch. My dad ended up finding it in his dresser drawer. He was always going through my dad's porn collection on his desk and stealing coins out of his coin jar. My dad probably would have killed my brother if my mother hadn't taken him. Reluctantly, my mother agreed, so my dad took my brother and met with my mom halfway, and that was it—my brother was gone. It was just my sister and I alone, stuck living with our pedophile father.

We were living in California, at this point I was about nine years old, and it was just the three of us. There wasn't a whole lot to do out there to keep us busy other than exploring the desert, building forts, swimming, jumping on the trampoline, riding four-wheelers, and other outdoor activities. Everything was so different, being there, just the three of us. The only good thing was that my brother was no longer there for Dad to slap around. Even though my brother treated me like crap and acted like he was going to kill me several times, I feel like I can't blame him for everything. I know he has some issues emotionally and all, but honestly, if he'd had different parents from the beginning to help him, I think he would be in a much better place now, emotionally, mentally, and financially. I kind of feel that he was just a victim of his surroundings as well.

I still spent a lot of time at the neighbors' house. Out of all of the kids, my sister and I had to grow up pretty fast. Even when my mom was there, we'd had a lot of chores, and we were learning how to cook and how to do laundry and things of that nature. However, when my mom left, my sister and I were completely in charge of making sure the entire house was in order, including my dad's clothes and his room.

My dad's job took up a lot of his time, so my sister and I were home alone quite a bit, especially in the summer when we weren't at school. We never really stayed at our friends' houses that much either. We would try to escape to our friends' houses as much as we could, but Dad didn't like it. I don't know if it was out of fear of us telling someone, or if it was a control thing. He never liked us staying at other people's houses, and we really didn't like inviting our friends over. Personally, I was afraid the night version of my dad would show up while they were there. I was afraid he would do something to them, or to me in front of them. I truly didn't like people staying the night at my house.

Dad had more parties with people over playing poker. Most of the people there were good people who truly seemed to care about me and my sister, but also seemed to have no idea what kind of person my dad actually was. He would have his parties, and he would go to bars, come home late at night, and come into my room.

I could always smell the liquor on him. I feel like that's what woke me up most of the time—not what he was physically doing to me, but the smell.

I find it crazy how a young child who is faced with something so awful can adapt when they shouldn't have to. That's what I feel like I did—I adapted. When I would smell him, my mind would wake up, but I couldn't move. I was paralyzed with fear. Internally I would scream at myself. I would think, *Move! Move! I know he will leave if you move. You just need to do it.* And then my hand would twitch. I began to gain control over my body again, was able to wake up quicker. But I still wasn't able to wake up before he touched me.

My dad was awful. Even when his wife had slept next to him, he would get up in the middle of the night to go to my room. He would even touch me as I lay in their bed between them. She would be right next to me with her back facing me.

When she left, though, this became a weekly, if not daily, thing. Every night, I truly felt alone. I had no escape. I would see my friends and their parents and wish that I had that. I would wish I could just have a normal dad. Then again, to the public eye, my dad was a normal dad, so it also made me think about how many of my friends had "normal" dads that would transition into another person, just like mine did.

Part of me really hated her; I hated my mom for leaving. I always thought she knew, and if she knew, how could she leave me there with him? How selfish could a mother be to leave your children with an abusive man? It really does make me sad admitting this, but I hated her more than I hated him. I used to wish he would remarry so I could have a mom that loved me and that would be there for me. I shouldn't have gotten my hopes up.

There's a lot of that time span—when it was just the three of us in California—that I've pushed back so deep in my memory that I feel like I've forgotten most of it, and sometimes those memories come back as nightmares. Anyone who knows my story tells me how brave I was, how strong I was, but when I look back, I feel like I was such a coward. *Why do I let him do these awful things to me? Is something wrong with me?*

SEVEN

usually find myself wondering: if my mom hadn't left, would he have stopped; would he have done everything he did. I know I can't blame her for what he did, I know that; but I can't help but blame her for leaving. Before she left, he would still come in my room at night; but after she left, not only did he come in my room every night, but he got more comfortable and less scared of me waking up.

There was a night that I woke up, and I could feel that my panties were off and my legs wide open. I instantly started screaming internally, *Move! Get up!* But I couldn't. I was stuck. Frozen in place. I then felt my dad between my legs and his hot breath on my vagina. My stomach was in knots; I felt I was going to throw up. Then I felt his tongue. I tried so hard to move—a toe, a finger, anything. I couldn't, and it felt like an eternity. Then the bile that was in my stomach rose to my throat, and I started coughing. Finally! My dad jumped up, threw the blanket on me, and left the room.

With time, it all got worse. It was a few weeks after my brother left to go live with my mom that my dad started doing more. It was a normal school night and I was in bed. I fell asleep, and I woke up with my father's penis on my lips. It was wet and cold. Once again, I was paralyzed. I couldn't move. Then I felt his fingers trying to open my mouth, and right when I felt his finger between my teeth, I was able to move my face away, making noises like I was slowly waking up. I rolled over, but I could feel him standing there staring at me. I stayed perfectly still out of fright. I was so damn scared that I lay there silently crying while he just stared at me. I couldn't move. I had to make him think that I didn't know what he was doing. He finally walked out of my room, and he went to his room and slammed his door shut as if he were mad.

The next night, my sister asked me if I wanted to sleep with her. I was so excited. "Yes, of course I want to," I said. He won't do it in bed with my sister. He wouldn't dare come in our room. When my dad came in and saw me in my sister's bed, he got mad and yelled at me, saying I was too old to be sleeping with her and to go back to my bed. My heart sank. I went to the bathroom and turned the bathroom sink on while I threw up in the toilet. My nerves got the best of me. I was extremely nervous of what he was going to do, now that I was alone again. He always had to be in charge, had to have complete power over us.

Over the next few weeks, Dad would come into my room at night and again take a piece of my innocence. Sometimes my sister would wake up and he would leave. Sometimes I would wake up. This one night I didn't. I remember waking up, and my panties were to my ankles and I didn't have a blanket on—completely exposed. I pulled my panties up and held myself crying, pinching my arm to hurt myself, like I was punishing myself for not waking up. All I could think about was, *What did he do to me?*

My dad, I believe, got tired of my sister helping me in that way. So, he started making me sleep in his bed. I wanted to talk to her about it, beg her to help me. I was ashamed, like it was my fault somehow. I was embarrassed. I never talked to her about it, and

I would think, *What can we do? We are just little girls. No one will believe us.*

I felt like I had no choice. So I would just go to his room and sleep there like he told me to do. I hated myself for it, like I was putting myself in the situation. I just didn't know what to do. What should I say? No. I was so scared of him. I had seen what he did to my brother. So I would do as he said and sleep in his room with him.

The first night he didn't do anything to me. I was extremely shocked, but I was so relieved at the same time. I thought, *Is it over? Is he done doing this?*

The next time he made me sleep in his room showed me I was wrong. I was asleep, but I woke up and felt like I was choking but couldn't cough. I heard him groan, and I felt like I was going to throw up. His penis was in my mouth. It felt like an hour had gone by with him moving slightly in my mouth. I was able to twitch my leg and then my hand. I know he saw my leg move because he stopped moving. Then he started again. I moved my hand and he stopped, pulled his boxers up, and lay down with his back to me. I opened my eyes and rolled over. I tasted something disgusting on my lips and teeth, like salt. I wiped it with my hand and wiped my hand on my shirt, moving very slowly so he didn't know what I was doing. I stayed awake the rest of the night. He got up early and left for work. I lay in my father's bed that smelled like his soap and cigarettes. I felt like a ton of bricks. I couldn't find the strength to move. I was eleven years old. I'd never even kissed a boy or had a boyfriend. I hated myself.

After a few months of him making me sleep in his room a few times a week, the unthinkable happened. The last night I was in his room was also the first time I felt his penis between my legs. I remember feeling this heavy weight on top of my body, and I remember hearing what sounded like someone spitting. As my mind started waking up more, I smelled his soap mixed with cigarettes.

He was on top of me, and he used his fingers to touch my vagina. His fingers were cold and wet. I tried to move, but I couldn't. I was constantly screaming internally, clawing at my insides to get out, to wake up. That's when he put his penis between my legs, making sure not to penetrate. Then I felt this warmth all over—I'd peed. I was so terrified that I actually peed myself.

He jumped up, pulled my pants up, and went to the bathroom. He came out, shook me, and said, "Felicity, wake up! Get up! You just wet the bed." He then told me to go change and go to sleep in my room.

I was awake the whole night crying silently. I couldn't move. I didn't even change. I lay there all night in piss filled clothes and cried until my cheeks burned. After that, he didn't make me sleep in his bed again until years later, when I'd stopped wetting the bed.

EIGHT

My dad and his friends liked to play poker all night. Other times, Dad would go to the bar. Nights that he went to the bar, he would come home at about two in the morning, most of the time with a woman. He would wake us up sometimes to come meet the woman he brought home, as if she were going to be our new mom or something.

This one time he went to the bar, he came home very late at night, drunk of course, with a lady named Rachel. He woke me and my sister up to come meet her and said she was making fried chicken. Rachel told me she'd always wanted daughters and that she could be our new mom.

I always hoped that he would find a woman. I always thought if he found a woman he would stop touching me. There were plenty of women he brought home, but he never stopped coming into my room at night. Rachel stayed the night that night, and yet he still came into my room. I woke up with my pants and panties to my ankles once again, awake but unable to move. It had started out with him just touching me with his hands, but now he had progressed.

Like that night, he touched me where a father should never touch his daughter—he touched my vagina. I woke up and his finger was inside me. It felt like I was being scratched on the inside. When I finally was able to move, I started by moving side to side, like I was slowly waking up. He hurriedly pulled my pants up, but only halfway because he was drunk. He covered me up and ran out of the room. I lay there not knowing if my sister was awake. I slowly pulled my pants all the way up and turned over. I sobbed but no sound came out. I silently cried every night for most of my life as a young girl.

I remember being so confused. I loved him—he was my dad, and during the day, he was a good enough dad. However, at night he was a monster that made me hate my life. He made me wish I wasn't alive. There were so many nights like that.

He used to drink all the time. When my mom was there, he would come into my room sober most of the time. When my mom left, he came into my room sober sometimes and drunk sometimes. Later on in my life, he used that as an excuse, actually. After he came into my room that night, with Rachel in his bed, I realized that his having another woman wouldn't change anything.

Dad actually dated Rachel for a couple of months. He brought us to her house for dinner. I remember she showed us this room high up in this tower building she had. She also made these amazing baked apples that she put ice cream in. Rachel wasn't bad, she was actually nice. A little weird, but nice. She was much older than my dad. I am pretty sure she was old enough to be his mom. They didn't last long though. Rachel wasn't the only woman—there were many.

Another one I remember was Taylor. She was really young and pretty. Dad brought us to her house a few times. Her house was a duplex—a really nice duplex. I remember Taylor took us to get candy, and she told me she was nervous that her boyfriend had two daughters. Taylor said she would do whatever she could to make sure we were comfortable. Once again, she didn't last long.

The next woman was Cynthia. I loved her and so did my sister. She lived in Tennessee. My aunt and uncle in Tennessee introduced her to my dad. She came to visit a few times. She was so beautiful and even more loving. Cynthia was your typical southern belle—so sweet, charming. Her hair and makeup always looked great. She had two older sons, who were also really nice. They were young adults and were away working or with friends most of the time. Cynthia was a real motherly figure, a mother I wish I'd had. I used to wish they would marry so she could be our stepmom. She truly did care about my sister and I, I could feel it. She had such a good aura around her. Dad and Cynthia actually got pretty serious. At this point, my dad was retired from the military, so he decided we would move to Tennessee.

NINE

Moving to Tennessee and leaving California behind was difficult. I had lived in the desert my whole life. All my friends were there. I believe my sister was even more upset than I was. Even though we were both upset, it was inevitable that the movers would still come.

The military was paying for my dad's move, so they sent packers. They packed every single item. I even had a bag of sugar and Kool-Aid powder in my room that we would eat as if it were candy, and I watched them wrap that up and pack it. We watched as they packed our whole lives into those boxes. Saying goodbye to my friends and neighbors was hard. I thought we would be friends the rest of our lives, but people drift apart, unfortunately.

The three us, my dog, Bruno, and my sister's cat all packed into the Nissan Pathfinder and started our drive to Tennessee. We stopped a few times on the way—bathroom and gas breaks, sightseeing, and time for Dad to take a nap since we were driving straight through.

Then we arrived in Tennessee at my aunt and uncle's house. My uncle and Dad were brothers. Their house was immaculate. They were huge Christians and so was my uncle's daughter, my cousin. It seemed good living there, to be honest. My sister and I shared a room upstairs with our own entrance to a shared bathroom. We were pretty excited about it.

I made friends with the neighbor, Anna. She was my age, and we became best friends pretty quick. She was fun and happy, something opposite to what I had grown used to feeling. Her parents were really nice and funny as well; they had a great sense of humor. Their house was huge and beautiful, and the yard was connected to my uncle's yard. I used to play with her every day on the trampoline or in their pool.

After a few days of staying there and my dad not coming into my room at night, I began to feel something I hadn't felt in a long time—I was actually happy. I was thinking that maybe the move was what he needed, so now he wouldn't do this to me anymore. I was hoping we could stay there forever, or at least awhile.

Unfortunately, it wasn't too long before Dad found a house for us. The house was old and on a dead-end street. It was three different colors; it was a cream color on top, a yellowish color in the middle, and an orangish-brown color on the bottom, all in three perfect horizontal lines. The house had these concrete steps and iron railings going to the front door. It had a basement that was attached to the garage and a big backyard. I remember getting there and letting the dogs out in the backyard for the first time. We had our chocolate Lab, Snickers, and my Rottweiler mix, Bruno. We had to find homes for our other dogs. I hated that we couldn't bring them all. I loved them. Those dogs always made me feel better, made me feel safe. Bruno and Snickers were curious and nervous at the same time. I just stood there watching them, and my dad came to stand beside me and put his arm around my shoulders.

In this house I had my own room. My room was next to my sister's, and Dad's room was at the end of the small hallway. It was nothing like the house we had in California. We started unpacking our rooms, and I found the bag of Kool-Aid powder that I'd seen the packer wrap in brown paper months before. I remember laughing that he'd packed that. Then I noticed the door had a lock on it. I got so happy knowing I could lock my door now.

The first night in the house didn't seem too bad. We said goodnight and headed to our rooms. I locked my door and got into bed. A little while after, I heard my doorknob turn; I was awake still. Then I heard my dad yelling to open the door right now. I jumped up and opened the door. He asked me why I had locked my door. I just told him I must have done it by accident. He said not to lock it again just in case there was an emergency and he had to get me. I agreed and said goodnight once again, knowing damn well why he didn't want the door locked.

My dad didn't come back in my room that night. I was so relieved at that moment, but the feeling didn't last long. He came into my room the next night, only this time I wasn't awake when he came in. I woke with his body on my back. I was lying on my stomach and my pants and panties were pulled all the way down. His penis was between my legs again, and it was wet with his spit. He smelled of cigarettes and whiskey. I felt like I was going to throw up. He grabbed my wrist tightly as if he were holding me down. I was able to move my leg a little, and he jumped off and ran out of the room like the coward he was. This time, it took me a little bit to fully wake and be able to move. My whole body felt like I was being held down. I felt so heavy.

Every time he did this to me, I felt a piece of me die. Hatred was growing inside me; I would feel anger and disgust, but not at him, at myself. I was so disgusted with myself. I hated my life and everything about me. I would catch myself thinking, *What did I do to cause this?* After beating myself up, I would flip the switch and put on a normal little girl face like nothing was wrong. I was really good at hiding my pain and hatred.

I woke the next morning, and he had already gone to work. My sister and I got ready for school and headed to the bus stop. The school itself wasn't too bad. Everyone seemed nice enough. The teachers were nice, and most of the students were OK. The school was huge and easy to get lost in.

I noticed this group of girls in my grade that were sticking together. They sat together in every class and at lunch. They seemed kinda rude to be honest. One of them spoke to me after a couple of weeks, her name was Sydney. When I first saw her and saw how she was acting, I didn't like her; I didn't want to be a part of her group. But when we started talking, I realized we actually had a lot in common. She was being raised by her grandmother, and neither of her parents were in the picture very much. I started hanging out with her and her friends.

When we got home, it was homework and chores time. Chores had to be done before Dad got home or else he would flip out. That's how our days usually went, at least until we got to know some of the kids in our neighborhood. We actually made friends with some kids on our street. Tennessee was starting to look like an OK place to live.

TEN

The neighborhood we moved to was nice. All the houses were close together, which we weren't used to at all. We went from having a couple of neighbors on one street to at least ten.

There was a family that lived at the end of our street—a mom, a dad, and their sons—and they were really into racing. Even their oldest son would drive and race on the track. The dad had this old Chevelle that was such a beautiful car. It was still in the middle of restoration, but he was extremely proud of that car. The mom was so nice and motherly; she said we were welcome there anytime.

We used to go down there and play video games, watch television, and play outside. Their mom always invited us over for lunches and dinners. I would help her clean and organize her house, and she was always so grateful. Once I said something about needing to paint my nails, and the mom said, "Oh my gosh, I can help with that." She was so excited. I let her paint my nails, and we talked about how she'd always wanted a daughter, but after her last son, she'd had two miscarriages and decided she was going to stay a boy mom. They always treated us so well, ever since the day we moved there.

Other than seeing the family down the street and a couple of kids in the neighborhood, we stayed in the house a lot. We used to walk to the apartment complex and play on the playground. The complex was right next to the neighborhood we lived in.

Sometimes, while Dad was at work, we would have friends over and not tell him. We would all just hang out, watch TV, and talk, and then they would leave before Dad got home. My sister snuck in a boy once when my dad was working overnights, and they went in her room. She was a teenager. She locked her door, and I was being the annoying little sister, sitting in the hallway kicking her door. She got extremely upset with me.

I loved when my dad worked overnights; it was only for a few months, but for those few months, he didn't come in my room. I actually slept really well. Knowing he wasn't in the house gave me all the peace I needed. He would get home in the early hours, but I would make sure I was awake before he got home. He ended up getting a new job, one where he would be home at night. Part of me believes that the only reason he got a new job was so he could continue business as usual. Sure enough, everything went back to normal. My version of normal anyways, where I would get the unwanted monster in my room every night.

My dad and Cynthia were still dating. She lived kind of far away from where we moved, so we would drive to see her every now and then with Dad and stay the weekend at her house. We had this one Christmas with her that I will always remember. She showed me and my sister how to make this breakfast casserole the night before so it would be really easy to just pop it in the oven the next morning. It was delicious. She brushed my hair that night and put it up in a ponytail. For the first time in a long time, I felt like I had a mom.

That evening we all watched a movie in the living room. Dad never came to me at night when Cynthia was around. The next morning we woke up and started opening presents. She got me and my sister these really cute sweat-suit outfits from Aeropostale, and I got this big stereo system. It was the best Christmas we'd had in a long time. I remember that night—dinner with everybody. Dad and she were on her back patio, and she was sitting on Dad's lap, and they were just loving on each other. I remember thinking, *I hope they get married. Maybe she can help me.*

I was really young at this time, and I don't really remember everything; I probably wasn't told everything either. But I do know that, years before, Cynthia had lost her first husband. He'd unexpectedly passed away, and it had really hurt her and her sons. I think it had a hold on her still. She ended up breaking up with Dad. My sister and I were so sad. We really did love her; she was the closest thing to a mother that we had at this point. She told me she would always be in our lives, and if we ever needed anything, she would be there. I don't know if it was me being desperate or nice, but I actually believed her. Turns out, that was a lie. We never saw her again.

After Cynthia, Dad became worse—more angry and drunk, more often than before. He started going to the lady across the street from us that lived alone. She was Dad's age. We didn't hang out with her much, but I know my dad went over there quite often. Anytime she saw us, she was really nice to me and my sister though. He didn't really have any other serious relationship after Cynthia. There was also never another woman whose presence would make my dad stop touching me.

ELEVEN

I f I wasn't depressed before, I definitely was now. After Cynthia left, everything seemed to get worse. Daytime dad wasn't as nice as he used to be. He was always talking down to us and making us self-conscious. Dad would always comment on our weight or our clothes. I use to wear sweaters that were three sizes too big for me; I was so self-conscious. No matter what I did, it was never good enough. If I gained a little weight, he would say I was getting fat. Then I would lose a little weight, and he would say that I needed to eat. It was a lose-lose.

He would also get mad over everything. We got home early one day, and we went down the street to the neighbors. Then we saw his car pull up, and we knew we were in trouble because our chores weren't done yet. My sister and I started running to the house, but it was too late. Dad was on the front steps throwing every single dish that was in the kitchen down to the yard; all the while he was yelling and cussing. All this because we didn't do the dishes before he got home. We thought we had time to do them, but he'd gotten home early. Everyone on our street saw him doing this. It was so embarrassing and demeaning. My sister and I picked up all the dishes, went inside, and got yelled at. He screamed at us, saying things like we were lazy and only cared about our friends. He was always like that—if it wasn't done when he wanted it done then it was a huge issue.

I forget what they were arguing about, my sister and dad, but they were arguing, and she slammed her bedroom door. The next day she came home to a doorless bedroom. He took it right off the hinges, and then he grounded her.

He always seemed to know things that we hadn't said to him; things we would only say to our friends on the phone. Mostly things about my sister and a boy she liked at the time, or things her friends would say to her. I always thought he was listening to my phone calls. Back then we had a house phone with no cord, but Dad didn't want us talking to people so long or in private, so he got a different phone. He got us the house phone with the long cord so we could take it into the living room or into the kitchen. Sometimes, when I was on the phone, he would be on the other line and say it was time to get off. The thing was, I never actually heard him get on in the first place. It was like he was listening from the start.

Every time he would go on one of his rants and be a jerk, I would find myself thinking about my mom. I would always wonder if she would be like him or if she would protect us from him. Then I would stop daydreaming and remember she left. She left us with him, and we hadn't spoken to her in years.

Every holiday, every birthday, I would find myself thinking of my mom. I had a sliver of hope that she would come and rescue us from the monster we called Dad. Years went by without even a call from her. I started to feel anger build up more and more.

After years of thinking like that, it finally happened—she reached out to us. I'm not exactly sure in what time of year it happened, but I know there were no holidays around that time. My sister and I received this big huge box in the mail; it was from my mom. It was the first thing we'd gotten from her since I was eight; I was twelve years old now. The box was filled with a bunch of Avon samples that she'd collected. My sister and I were shocked and happy at the same time, but yet really confused. That's when Dad told us we were going to stay with her in New York for a couple of weeks, and my brother was going to come to Tennessee to be with him. I felt torn about how I should feel. I didn't exactly know her, but at that time, I didn't really like her either. I remember thinking, *Well, at least she won't be worse than Dad.*

I hated him and I hated my life. I still had these dark clouds following me. I was excited to see my mom but also quite bitter. The day he told us we were going to see my mom, I wrote my plans in my binder. I always wrote in my binder—plans to run away, plans to kill myself, and plans to kill him. I decided to write it in a school binder because if I'd had a diary he would read it. He never checked my school books, and honestly, I didn't think anyone would. I would write very detailed plans in this binder. When I started writing in the binder in California, it was mostly about how to kill myself. Would I use a razor blade? Could I shoot myself with one of my dad's guns? Maybe just take a lot of pills that were in his medicine cabinet. As time went on and I got older, I started planning my escape—how to run away and ideas of where I would go. I even wrote goodbye letters to my sister and to my dad. My letter to Dad was quite hateful. I will always remember this one thing I said to him in every letter: I wrote, "Dad, you are the monster I wish would be hunted and tortured. You are a despicable piece of shit that deserves to be thrown out like trash."

In California, running away was unrealistic; we were too far away from everything. But in Tennessee, we were closer to everything. I used to think about stealing the money in his change jar and finding a way to a bus stop. I would buy a ticket and go to Florida. I used to dream about living on the beach and swimming every day. I had no idea of where I would live or how I would live, but I just felt like being away from this life would make it all worth it.

Plans of killing myself turned into plans of running away, then morphed into plans to kill my dad. I felt like it was a daydream, thinking about killing him. We had rat poison under the sink in the kitchen. I thought about putting some in his whiskey. How long would it take him to die? Could he hurt me and my sister before he died from the poison? Then I thought about putting the sleeping pills that he had in his medicine cabinet into the whiskey, with hopes that it would knock him out and I could suffocate him. It got to the point where I had so many doubts about whether I could do it or not. Then I thought maybe I could just shoot him in his sleep.

I was home alone one day—my dad was at work, and my sister was at her friends. I opened his gun safe. I picked up one of the guns and just held it for a minute. I put it to my head and just sat there. I started crying instantly, put the gun back, ran to the bathroom, and sat on the floor crying, hitting myself in the face and screaming; I felt like such a coward. Why couldn't I just pull the trigger? End my sorry excuse of a life? I wanted to kill myself, but, at times, it was more to punish him than to save myself from the torture. He got pleasure in molesting me, and if I died, I would be taking that pleasure away; so suicide was heavy on my mind.

Even with having all these plans, I stayed. All the plans of running away, plans to kill myself, plans to kill him—I couldn't do any of it. I was too scared. Too scared of what would happen if I failed. Scared of leaving my sister alone with him. I was always so scared, but I still craved death. Whether it was to punish him or to save myself, I wanted to die. I didn't want to be in this world and be the person I was. I was disgusted by my dad, but sometimes I was more disgusted with myself—I was so scared of the possible outcome and the what-ifs; I felt like a coward. I thought about telling so many times: telling a teacher, telling my friend Sydney's grandmother or my friend Anna's mom; I even thought about telling my aunt and uncle. But all I could think about was that no one would believe me.

No one.

TWELVE

We eventually ended up going to see my mom for those couple of weeks while my brother went to my dad. It was weird seeing her for the first time. She hugged us and kissed us; she even cried. I didn't feel anything toward her. I didn't feel the love or affection that a daughter usually has for her mother. I felt like she was a stranger. She kept bringing up things, memories she had. My sister and I would look at each other like "what is she talking about," not remembering any of it.

My mom was always acting. Sometimes I felt like she really believed all those lies she spoke about, like she was mother of the year. To this day I don't remember much from my childhood with her. My mom had her own issues. She wasn't financially stable or emotionally stable. Honestly, it was disheartening. She wasn't someone who I felt could give me the life of a kid who is loved and happy. I would look at her, then think of my dad, and couldn't help but feel this ever-growing doom, like "this is what I have as role models, as parents: a father who molests me every night and a mother too self-centered and mentally unstable to even notice that her children are in danger."

She was living in a trailer at a trailer park. There were so many kids, boys and girls, all around our age. We would just hang out in the park, and they would show us trails and fun stuff to do.

I became friends with this girl, who was a couple years older than me, named Vicky. Her family was weird but really nice. The house was cluttered all the time, and they had a lot of dogs. Vicky had this older brother named Adam. He kept smiling at me, always asking me questions. Every time he would walk by, he would put his hand on my lower back. I felt like what I was going through with my dad made me more aware of people's movements and motives— much more observant than your typical little girl.

I stayed the night at that girl's house. My sister was at my mom's. We stayed up for a while watching TV and talking. It came down to bedtime, and she was knocked out on the bed. I slept on a blow-up mattress on the floor. I was sitting there with my eyes open, wide awake, and her older brother, who was like twenty-eight or twenty-nine, walked by. He looked in her room and saw I was awake. He pointed to me and said, "Come here."

I got up; he was at the edge of the hallway by his door, waving me into his room. He asked me how old I was, and I told him, "I'm twelve." He said I looked much older than twelve years old.

He asked me if I wanted to sleep in his bed. I stayed silent for a moment, and he said, "If you don't want to, you can go back to my sister's room."

It was in that instant that I decided I was going to sleep with him. I knew what he wanted. As disgusting as it made me feel saying this, I wanted it to, but for different reasons than him. My dad took away so many firsts for me: my first kiss, the first time someone else touched my body, the first time I felt a penis on me. My dad stole my innocence. The one thing he hadn't stolen yet was my virginity. I wanted control of that, and I was afraid if I didn't act soon, my dad would steal that from me too. With everything my dad had done to me, he had never penetrated me with his penis, but I had a feeling he was going to try eventually. So right then and there I decided I was going to lose my virginity before my dad took it. I was going to lose it on my own terms.

I lay in his bed, and he got on top of me. He tried to kiss me, but I turned my head. I couldn't do it. I closed my eyes, and he pulled my pants down. He pushed himself inside of me. I remember feeling pain and feeling tears run down my cheek. Honestly, that's all I remember though. I don't remember it ever feeling good. I don't remember what he did or how he did it. I kept telling myself, *You did the right thing; you did the right thing; you did the right thing.*

It was finally over. He got up and asked me if I was OK. I said yes, and I went to the bathroom. I washed my face off, then sat on the toilet. I peed, and when I wiped, there was a little blood. I sat down on the bathroom floor crying with no sound coming out, tears just pouring out of my eyes. I didn't want to have sex with him. I didn't desire him. I just knew what he wanted from me, and I used that. I may have been crying, but I knew deep down my dad could never take that from me like he took everything else. I went back to my friend's room, lay on the air mattress, and cried silently until I fell asleep.

The next morning, her parents were making breakfast. Her brother was already gone, and I went home to my mom and sister. I didn't tell them anything. I didn't even act different. Having to hide what my dad had been doing to me my entire life made it easy for me to put on an act. I learned how to act like I was happy and unbothered. I could be so depressed and broken yet put a smile on my face. I can still do that to this day—the ultimate poker face. I always thought I needed to be strong for myself because no one else would be. It's tiring, to be honest, always being strong, with no one to lean on when you're feeling down. I was exhausted.

That day was a normal day: after some grocery shopping, we

cleaned. Every time my mom talked, I would get annoyed. I didn't feel anything for my mom. All I knew was that everything she said got on my nerves; I would question everything she said. I couldn't trust her.

My grandma and grandpa died when we were visiting my mom. I remember lying on the couch with my sister, crying about it. It was my dad's mother and stepfather; I loved them so much. They showed me what real love meant, what it was supposed to be. Grandma was always calling him sweetie and he always called her love. They were always joking and laughing with each other. I had always thought, *How did such a beautiful woman create such a monster.* I never thought about telling her. I couldn't build up the courage or the nerve. She loved my dad. She seemed so proud of him, and I loved her. I couldn't take that from her.

When we got back to my dad's, everything seemed to go back to normal at first. Then the second night we were home, I had a nightmare. It was a rerun of what happened with my friend's brother. It was dark, and the room looked like Adam's room. This male figure came to the bed, and I thought it was Adam; but then a sliver of light hit his face, and I saw that it was my dad. I woke up in a panic. I went to the bathroom and threw up. All I could think about was how disgusting I was. So, not only was my dad invading me in real life, but now he was invading my sleep and my dreams. I couldn't get away.

After about a week of being home, he started making me sleep in his room. I really didn't want to, but I just felt so stuck. What could I possibly do or say to get out of this, to make him not want me to be in there? It didn't matter what I did or how I acted. The attitude, the arguing, none of it mattered—he wanted me in his bed at night sleeping with him.

The first night I slept in his room, I woke up with his hot breath on my vagina. I felt like my body was nailed to the bed, unable to move, once again trapped in this prison—this hell. I remember his hand gripping my thigh to the point of it hurting. My mind was awake, but my body was asleep. My own father was touching me like a husband would touch his wife.

A couple nights a week, he would ask me to sleep in his room; he would have a threatening finality in his voice. He made it seem like I'd better not argue. The nights that I was in my bed, he would still come in the night. The only time I seemed to get any peace was when my dog, Bruno, was in my room, which was rare.

I tried to get Bruno to sleep in my room every night, but my dad didn't allow it. Bruno didn't like him, but that dog loved me. Dogs know who's bad and who isn't. I snuck Bruno in one night, and he was lying at the foot of my bed. He was right next to my door. My dad opened the door, and Bruno growled at him. My dad turned the light on and hit him. He got Bruno off the bed and threw him outside. He told me, "This is why you can't have a dog in your room! I refuse to have a dog growl at me in my own house!" and he slammed the door shut. Any bit of peace or security, my dad would take away instantly, like not being allowed to lock my door or being yelled at for the dog sleeping in my room. He just wanted complete control over me, and he had it.

THIRTEEN

Going to school in Tennessee was easier than when we'd lived in California. The teachers were way nicer, and the school was nice as well. I worked in the school store every morning. Students would come before class and use cash they earned from their classroom (like school cash). They would buy things like pencils, pens, erasers, notebooks, and journals.

I had this one teacher that I truly connected with; her name was Miss Mitchell. She wasn't married and had no kids. She was a huge baseball fan and loved the Orioles. She would talk to Sydney and I about life and how it could be hard sometimes, but you just needed to be resilient and push forward. I really enjoyed going to her class.

I did well in school. I got good grades; I behaved for the most part. I mean, I did get into a couple of fights, but it was nothing major. Becoming friends with Sydney kept my mind off things, which helped. She loved gossip, so she would always tell me who was dating whom, who had cheated on whom, who had been lying. She even knew about teachers, knew all types of stuff. I swear she knew everything that was going on in that school. We were inseparable during this time, at least while we were at school. We would even get a hall pass at the same time just so we could go to the bathroom together. Most of the time, we would just walk around the halls and talk.

When I started hanging out with Sydney, outside of school was where we got closer and became like best friends and not just school friends. I came to her house and met her grandmother. Her aunt lived across the street with her little cousin. At first glance, she had a perfect life—beautiful house, cool room, all the nicest clothes and shoes—but like every family, they had their problems too. Her grandmother was a saint though, and she always told me I was Sydney's "good" best friend—out of all her friends, I was the good one. Grandmother loved me and I loved her.

We used to sit at the kitchen table and do homework. We would talk and be silly. Grandmother would come home from work with a bag of hot Cheetos and two Dr Peppers because she knew they were our favorites. Dad actually liked Sydney and her grandmother, surprisingly. Dad always had an issue with anyone we hung out with, and he let those issues be known. He always talked badly about my sister's friends, always saying they were gay, fat, ugly, or weird. He was always so mean about her friends.

He didn't like us being away from the house often. I know that whenever I asked to go hang out or stay the night at a friend's place, he always made it out to be such a big deal. He would get so mad and yell if we didn't ask at least a week ahead of time. It didn't matter what we wanted to do—to go to the movies or the mall, or to stay the night at our friends'.

I also made friends with this girl named Ashley in our neighborhood. She was older than me. She was into things that I wasn't really into yet, like boys, relationships, smoking weed, drinking, and having sex. When I went to her house, it would be just Ashley, her older sister sometimes, her mom, and her little brother. We would always just hang out in her room talking. She would always ask me so many questions about what I liked and how I grew up.

After a few months, she asked me if I had a crush on somebody. I told her yeah, but he was a little older than me and probably didn't even know my name. That's when she told me that someone in her grade thought I was pretty. I asked her who, but she made me tell her the name of my crush first. His name was Alex. She started laughing so hard and said, "Holy crap, that's who likes you." I was instantly terrified. I'd never really been interested or had a crush on anyone before.

She called him and said that I wanted to hang out. I was sitting there telling her, "No, no, no, no, no, no, don't do that. Don't do that." She hung up the phone and said he wanted to meet me at the playground at the apartment complex. I was so nervous and scared. He was two years older than me. She asked me if I was going to kiss him. Besides the thing at my mom's, I had never hung out with a boy alone, let alone kissed someone.

I walked to the playground to meet him. We sat on the swings for a little while. He was just asking me a lot about myself. After about two hours, he asked me if I'd ever been kissed before. My heart instantly sank, and I thought about my dad kissing me. I felt disgusted, but I just told him, "No, I haven't."

He leaned in to kiss me, and I kissed him back; but as soon as he tried to put his tongue in my mouth, I almost threw up. Thoughts of what my dad had done to me that day in the car and what he'd done to me ever since came rushing forward. I told him, "I'm sorry I can't do this," and I ran away.

I ran home and threw myself in my bed, crying. My first crush. My first real kiss. It was ruined because of my dad, because of what he'd done to me all my life.

FOURTEEN

From an outsider looking in, I was a happy young girl, innocent. I was putting on an act, and it was so tiring on my mind, body, and soul. It was literally exhausting. I was so filled with shame and disgust. I felt like I had nobody to talk to—nobody to share my secrets with or to share my pain with. I felt I had no support from anyone to lighten the burden of my life. It was like I lived on an island and the only one that could come to the island was the monster that invaded my room at night.

I would think about ways to kill myself daily. I would lie in my bed wondering if I could do it. Tears would be streaming down my face, but no noise would come out. I felt like a coward all over again: a coward for being scared to wake up and tell her dad to never touch her again; a coward for not telling anybody about what was happening; a coward for not going through with my plan to kill myself.

I couldn't kill myself because of my sister. I even stood in the shower once with a razor to my wrist, but the only thing I could think of was that she would be the one to find me. I dropped the razor and lay in the bathtub, crying. At times I felt like going through with it would be easy, as if the most difficult thing I would ever have to do in my lifetime would be to not take my own life, but then I would think of my sister—of leaving her alone with him. So I fought to keep the will to live. To fight.

I felt like I would welcome death, but I was terrified of being the cause of the pain my sister would feel because of it. Growing up watching my mom do everything she could to stay and look young, listening to the women in my life—whether it was my dad's girlfriends, my teachers, or my friends' moms—talk about aging like it was a bad thing, everyone seemed to fear death; but I actually craved it at one point. I used to wish I could be braver and stronger so I could take that handful of Vicodin my dad had in his medicine cabinet or use that razor on my wrist in the shower.

I just hated myself. I hated my life. I wanted a way out. Running away wasn't an option: I didn't have any money; I didn't have anyone to go to. I would probably just get picked up by the cops and sent right back to the man that molested me every night. I felt like the only option I truly had was to kill myself. I used to hurt myself every time I felt this shame and disgust. I would slap myself, pinch myself, and even scratch myself until I bled. I used to have a hair tie on my wrist that I would snap over and over until my entire wrist would turn purple. I felt like it was the only thing I really had control over—control over my pain. I hated myself more than I hated my dad, at one point.

I would write all of these thoughts and plans in my binder. My plans of running away turned into plans of killing myself, and my plans of killing myself turned to plans of killing my dad. I only ever wrote about them in my binder. I never told anyone, not a soul, and no one ever saw them until the day I saw my sister holding that binder in the doorway of our kitchen.

My dad was at work, and we were doing chores in the house. I was in the kitchen doing dishes, and we had the music up loud listening to Dixie Chicks like we always did when we cleaned. She called my name; I looked over to the doorway, and there she was with my binder in her hands. She was crying, asking me why I hadn't told her.

At first I was angry, and I got mad at her for reading my binder. She dropped the binder and hugged me. We sat on that kitchen floor crying, holding each other. I don't know how long we stayed like that, but it felt like a long, long time. I told her I hadn't known for sure that she knew. She told me she hadn't known that I knew what was going on when I was sleeping. She asked me when I'd realized, or at least had an idea, that she knew what my dad was doing. I told her it was when our brother had read her diary to our friends. She instantly remembered that day. We cried even more, sobbing, and just holding each other like we'd been separated for years.

We spoke a little bit about what was going on but never in great detail. We were both very vague. Few memories were shared between the two of us. All I know is, once we both realized that the other knew, we became closer. I even started sleeping in her room again.

Her room was right next to Dad's, so we had to whisper so he couldn't hear us. Sometimes we would be joking and laughing so loud that he would yell at us to be quiet. I have to say, those were some of the best times in my childhood. We would laugh so hard that we would cry. Our cheeks would be swollen and sore from smiling. The best part was, when I was in her bed, Dad wouldn't come to mine.

A part of me thinks he knew what we were doing by my sleeping in her bed. He started fighting with us about it, saying we were too old to share a bed, even though he would make me sleep in his sometimes. He wanted to take everything from us—any bit of happiness or control we had in our lives, he would snatch away, like it was his. He started making it hard for me to sleep in her bed. After that I stopped thinking of killing myself or killing him, and I started thinking about telling on him, reporting him to someone—anyone.

A few months later, we were cleaning the house, and my sister needed to vacuum her room. Her outlet didn't work, so she went into my dad's room, which was right next to hers, to plug in the vacuum. She came running to me saying, "Felicity, come see this. I have to show you." She brings me to my dad's room and shows me this black box that's plugged into the wall and the phone. He was recording our calls.

We always wondered how he knew certain things, things that we might have only said while whispering on the phone to a friend. Once we saw that recorder, we knew that was how he'd done it all along. I was so mad—like everything he'd done to me my entire life wasn't enough, now he had to take away what little privacy I thought I had. Listening to me talk in private to my friends on the phone proved he literally wanted to take everything from us. It felt like the last straw, and I was fed up. That was when I made my decision.

I was going to tell on my dad.

FIFTEEN

I felt like I'd reached my breaking point. I know it sounds crazy that it took finding out he was recording our phone calls to reach the actual breaking point, but everything piled on top of each other, one after another, after another. He was taking a piece of my humanity and dignity every chance he got. I was fed up.

I told my sister one day that I was going to tell on him. She was terrified. She asked me, "Who are you going to tell?" I told her I didn't know yet, but it was going to happen, and I wanted her to be prepared. I ended up deciding the best way to do this was to use someone else's phone so it wouldn't be recorded on my dad's recorder. He came home from work, and I asked him if I could go to my friend Anna's house (she was the friend that had the backyard that was lined up with my aunt and uncle's backyard). He got a little mad at me because it was so last minute, but he ended up agreeing.

I called Anna and said I really needed to come over. Her mom came and picked me up. We went right into Anna's room. I told her I needed to use her phone to call my mom. She asked me why, and I told her my dad was molesting me and I needed to get me and my sister out of there. She was shocked; I'd never told her before. She went and got the phone without her mom knowing. I went into the closet, I shut the door, and I called my mom. I told her that Dad had been molesting me all my life, and now he was recording our phone calls. The first thing she said was, "Are you sure?"

I was instantly angry. I said, "What do you mean am I sure?" She said that was a big accusation, and she wanted to make sure that I was being honest. I yelled and said forget it; then I hung up on her. I threw the phone and cried.

Anna came in asking me what happened, and I told her what my mom said. She was in complete disbelief. Anna said, "How can your mom not believe you?" Then she asked me what I was going to do now. I said I didn't know, but I needed to go home to tell my sister. Her mom took me home, and I told my sister everything. We both just cried.

My dad came home for dinner, and I could see how uncomfortable my sister was. We didn't know what was going to happen.

Once he went back to work, I got a call from Anna's mom saying I forgot something at her house and she was coming over to bring it to me. My sister and I were so confused. We ran down the street to a neighbor's house to use their phone to call my mom; we needed to know what she had done. My mom had called the cops and Anna's mom, explained what I'd said, and asked if Anna's mom could come to my house.

My friend Anna came with her mom and her siblings. Her mom was crying and said she wished I would have told her sooner. She told us not to worry and that she would be here for us. When the cops arrived, I was terrified, and I instantly regretted telling on him. I didn't want him to go to jail. I didn't want him to get arrested. I just wanted him to get help, to stop what he was doing to me.

The Child Protective Services worker took my sister into a room alone and asked her questions. Then she took me in the room and started questioning me. I did not tell her anything in detail. I thought that if I told her a little, it would be enough to get us out of his care but not enough for him to be put in jail. I was young and ignorant; I didn't know how it worked. I should have told them everything.

When they were done questioning us, Anna and her family left. My aunt and uncle pulled into the driveway. We were told to pack our clothes and school stuff and that we were going to stay with next of kin, my dad's brother. That scared me though. All I could think about was "It's my dad's brother. He's going to be mad at me for saying this about Dad."

Once we got in the truck, they asked us if we were OK. We just said yes and stayed quiet. I asked how Dad was. My uncle said, "The cops went and told your dad at work what was happening, so he knows you guys are coming to stay with us."

I was relieved and sad at the same time. I knew we were all my dad had. I felt like he loved us. I loved him. He was all we had for a long time. I was so conflicted on how to feel. I couldn't help but think about his feelings. Will he be OK? Is he mad at me? I hated myself for thinking or even caring about his feelings, but I couldn't help it.

I was actually scared he would kill himself. I don't even know how to explain it, honestly. I know it sounds bizarre, but I was worried. I loved him still. The people that know what he did to me ask me, "How did you forgive him?" and my answer is the same now as it was then: I don't know. I feel like I was brainwashed into feeling what I thought was love for this monster. I wish I hadn't felt love; then all of this would have been so easy.

SIXTEEN

Living at my aunt and uncle's was bad and good at the same time. At first I felt like the good outweighed the bad. They had a beautiful house, a loving marriage, and they seemed happy. They were both Christians—they didn't go to church or anything, but they always praised God. My aunt's daughter, my cousin, she never missed church. They would have us go with her every week in hopes that we would be saved.

I've said it before: I didn't believe in God then, and I don't believe in God now. The entire time we were there, I felt like I was being force-fed this religion—belief in the Almighty, God is a great god, and everything happens for a reason. I still don't understand how people can believe this one man created all of life; that the all-powerful God allows awful things to happen all the time. For this exact reason, I am a non-believer. If he's so powerful, why doesn't he stop it? Why didn't he stop my dad coming into my room every night for years? Why didn't God save me or my sister?

Weeks went by, and we did the same thing over and over: go to school, come home, do our chores, eat dinner, play with the neighborhood kids for a little bit, and then shower and bed. My aunt was very particular about how we cleaned her house. Sometimes I felt like we were little maids. I think my aunt thought it was good for us. Even though I may have felt like a maid and felt like I was being forced into a religion I didn't believe in, it was still better than where we were before.

Some weekends when my aunt and uncle were gone, my sister and I would have all the windows wide open for fresh air. We would blast Dixie Chicks while we cleaned. We both loved to sing, and I'm sure the neighbors could hear us singing along. It was one of the times that I felt like a normal kid and like I had a normal life.

One evening I got a call from Anna. She was down the street at this girl Jessica's house. Anna sounded weird, and she asked me if I could come get her. I went into the living room and asked my aunt and uncle if I could go hang out with Anna. They told me it was fine and to be home by eight.

I ran down to Jessica's house and knocked on the door; two older guys answered. One was Jessica's older brother and one was his friend. I walked in and found out Jessica was upstairs with a guy and Anna was on the couch between three guys—she looked drunk.

I asked her if she was OK, and she slurred her words, saying "No, I need to go home." All the guys were trying to get her to stay and trying to get me to stay.

I helped her off the couch and said, "Her parents are looking for her; we have to go," and they let us go. I had to help her walk all the way up the street and up this huge hill to her house. I was holding her up, and I asked her what had happened, what was wrong with her? She said she smoked weed with them, but she thought they put something else in it, and she felt really weird. I told her I was so glad she'd called me, because there's no telling what those guys would have done to her. Then I called her stupid. I told her Jessica wasn't a good person, and her brother just wanted to hang out with them like it was cool, like he wasn't too old for them. All she did was agree and say she was sorry.

I got her to her house, up the stairs, and into her bed. I covered her up so she could sleep it off, and I went home. I walked in the door, and my uncle was on the couch watching TV. My aunt and sister were on the other couch. I came in and sat with my uncle. He asked me how it had gone, and I said it was fine, thanks for letting me go. He said it was no problem and started watching his show again. I said I was going to take a shower and get ready for bed. Everyone seemed fine. After my shower I lay down in bed and fell asleep.

I woke up the next morning and my sister was already downstairs. I got up, stretched, brushed my teeth, and headed downstairs. I saw my sister, aunt, and uncle at the kitchen table in the dining room. He asked me to sit. I sat down, but I was confused; they looked so mad and my sister was crying.

My uncle started yelling at me, telling me he could tell that I was high last night. I started to tell him no I wasn't, but he just yelled more. He and my aunt berated me and made me feel as tiny as an ant. They kept saying things like I was no good; I was going to hell; I would be pregnant by fifteen. They said they couldn't have me living there being a bad influence on my sister. I was sick, sick to my stomach. They were kicking me out, making me leave my sister. They yelled at me to go pack my bag. My sister was still crying at the table. I packed my bag and came downstairs. My uncle said to go get in the truck.

I started walking down the driveway, and Anna's mom's van was parked at the end of the driveway. My uncle was right behind me. The window went down on the passenger side of the front seat of the van. It was Anna, her dad, mom, and her siblings. Her dad yelled at me. He said he knew I was going to be a bad influence on his daughter and how dare I do that to her—how dare I make her smoke and force her. My stomach sank to the ground. I thought she was my best friend, but she lied to save her own ass. She threw me under the bus and acted like the whole thing was on me.

That's when I started to crumble. I thought she was my best friend. I lied to my aunt and uncle so I could go help her, and there she was, sitting in the back seat of the van with her head down. Her parents yelled, and all the while my uncle stood behind me with a disapproving look on his face. Everyone thought that I was the troubled one, but little did they know, or believe, that I'd never done a drug or gotten drunk.

After they were done yelling at me, they drove off quickly. My uncle snatched my bag off my back and threw it in the truck. He told me to get in. I asked him where we were going, and he said, "Somewhere where you belong."

He drove me to this place called the Crisis Center. As soon as you walked in, there was this little sitting area and then a room shaped like an octagon full of glass windows. It was in the middle of the house—they could see everything through the windows.

A worker and a therapist came out to greet us. They made me open my suitcase and told me I could only bring three shirts, three pants, three pairs of socks, and three sets of night clothes. No razors, but I was allowed a brush and a toothbrush. Once I picked everything out, they zipped up my suitcase and took it away. They asked my uncle why he was bringing me there, and he told them that I was a child of sexual abuse. He told them I was doing drugs and lying to him. He said they couldn't let me live at their house and be a bad influence on my sister.

They had my sister wrapped around their finger. She loved them, but I could see right through them. They were hypocrites: living as Christians, speaking about forgiveness, but then screaming in my face, telling me I would be nothing; yelling at me, saying I was just like my mother and that I was going to hell. True believers of God talking to a fourteen-year-old girl like that—what kind of Christians were they?

They started telling my uncle how it worked there, telling him I would have to get checked for STDs and drugs. He told them to do whatever they needed to do, and he left.

The next morning they took me to an ob-gyn. It was my first time seeing one. They made me pee in a cup, and the doctor gave me a pap smear. Later that evening the worker brought me into the office and asked me if I'd ever done drugs. I told him no and that my uncle and aunt didn't believe me. They called my uncle on speaker and told him that I'd tested negative for drugs. There was silence. Then he said he didn't care and he hung up. I was stuck there. I literally had no one.

This place was meant for kids that had no one and were troubled. They believed they could help these children, but the reality was the exact opposite.

They had this long hallway in the home. On one end was the boys' room and on the other end was the girls' room. If you stood in the doorway of the room, you could see the door at the end of the hallway, but the workers in the middle of the room couldn't see you as long as you stayed in the doorway. One day, in the first week of being there, I sat in my bed and watched girls flashing the boys and the girls giggling when the boys would flash them back. They did this almost every night.

We would be watching movies where the boys and girls could share blankets. I remember seeing a blanket move up and down while one of the girls was giving a boy a hand job. This place wasn't helping anyone.

After a week or so, I started going to their school. There was this classroom where we all went, but I needed to get my schoolwork. Two of the workers took me to my actual school and let me go to my classes to get my work and books. None of the teachers really said anything to me except for Miss Mitchell. She asked me if I was OK, told me how sorry she was—sorry that she didn't know—and how she wished she could have helped. She told me that she would be there if I ever needed her.

The therapist I had was really kind; she would take me for walks in Nashville, over by a college and to the parks. We would just walk and talk. She would tell me I could talk to her about anything I wanted. I told her I wasn't going to talk to her about my dad, and she said she completely understood. She never pushed me. I remember this one walk through the Garden of Great Ideas on a college campus. There was this sculpture called "Memory Return" that I felt a pull toward. It was of an older woman and child. It was symbolic of memories being the end and having a cycle. I told the therapist that I thought I had ended the cycle that plagued my entire life. She told me that I would be OK; that I was one of very few children she would meet with that she felt comfortable saying that to. She said I was strong enough to get through anything, that I was strong enough to overcome difficulties, and that she believed me.

At the Crisis Center, we would get up early, around 5 a.m., and we all had chores to do, one of which was cooking for all the kids in the center. We also had allotted phone times where we could call friends or family. The first week, I called my sister every day, but I only got to speak to her once or twice before my aunt and uncle realized. I started to speak to Sydney almost every day after that. Her grandmother always asked me if I was being fed or if I needed anything. I felt a great sense of love from that woman. She would tell me I was strong, that I could get through anything. I know my sister wanted to be there for me, but my aunt and uncle made it very hard for her to be. Sydney and her grandmother were there for me, made me feel not so alone.

Then all of our bunk beds at the center ended up getting

termites. The workers called the children's caregivers and told them that they needed to be picked up by that Friday at five or else they would be put into foster care. My mom assured them that she would be there. Friday came and we all started packing our things and saying our goodbyes. All the kids were picked up way before five. Then the clock turned to 5 p.m. and what do you know, no Mom. The therapist looked at me and said, "Your mother said she's on her way, so I will wait with you for as long as it takes."

We sat in her car listening to music, talking about nothing important, and at about 8:30 or 9 p.m. I saw lights turning into the driveway. My mom got out of the car, ran to me, and hugged me. It felt like a stranger was hugging me. She kept apologizing about being late, and she told me to leave my bag for a second, that she would get it. She introduced me to her boyfriend, who had driven with her.

Then I saw him—my dog. Bruno was in the backseat of her car. I ran to him and hugged him so tightly. He kept licking me and I just cried. My mom told me she had gone to my dad's first to get my dog. Knowing that, I forgave her instantly for being so late. I remember thinking, *Maybe she does care about me.* I gave my therapist a hug. Then my mom and I headed to New York.

SEVENTEEN

The drive to my new home in New York was strange to say the least. Mom kept talking as if she'd been in my life this whole time. Her boyfriend spoke to me like he knew everything about me. I was in the car with two strangers; but I had my dog. I'd had Bruno since he was a puppy. For years this dog was my protector. He didn't like Dad much, and he would growl at him often. My dad would always yell, saying he was going to make me get rid of him because he refused to have a dog in his house growl at him. When I saw him in the car and heard my mom say that she'd picked him up first, I literally cried. I did not want to leave him in Tennessee, and especially didn't want to leave him with my dad.

It was a long drive to New York, but when we got there, Mom went inside and put her dog in her room and showed me where Bruno and I would sleep. She said the next day we would introduce our dogs to make sure they would get along.

My brother definitely didn't want me there; even his hug when we first arrived was forced. He knew why I was there, and he hated me even more. How dare I say those things about his hero, our father. He always acted as if Dad could do no wrong. His number one goal in life was to make Dad proud of him. It's sad to say that I don't think my dad has it in him to ever say he's proud of his son.

I went to bed with Bruno, and I actually slept well. I didn't even feel the need to lock the door. The next day Mom said she wanted to introduce our dogs. I got up and got dressed. I brought Bruno outside, and when we came back in, Mom had her dog on a leash. Her puppy was six or seven months old, but he was huge and bigger than Bruno already. He was a Great Dane mix. So there we were in the living room, and Mom brings Argus over to Bruno. Bruno didn't do anything except stand very still. Argus came over, stood over him, and growled. Then Bruno growled. Argus snapped at Bruno and Bruno jumped on him. Mom and her boyfriend broke up the fight that erupted between Argus and Bruno. I was crying; Mom was crying. It was a mess.

Mom yelled, saying, "I can't get rid of my dog, Felicity!"

I screamed back, "Your dog was aggressive first! Your dog!"

I brought Bruno into my room and lay in bed crying while I held him. I knew she was going to make me get rid of Bruno. I was devastated. After a while I went into the living room, and Mom was crying already. Right then I knew I was right. She said that she couldn't get rid of her puppy, that she loved him too much. She started talking about the Humane Society, and how it's so good for helping dogs find a home.

I zoned out, not listening anymore. I was shocked. I had been here for one day, and my mom had already broken any bond we might have had before it even started to form. I'd had Bruno for *years*. She'd only had her puppy for six or seven months at this time. She was so selfish. My mom didn't even think twice or ask how I felt. She said what was happening, and I had no choice.

We got in the car. I sat in the back with Bruno. It was complete silence on the way to the Humane Society. You could cut the tension with a knife—that's how I felt and I knew she felt it. I don't think she cared as long as she didn't have to get rid of her beloved puppy.

Once inside the facility, the workers asked my mom questions, as if she knew anything about my dog. She had the audacity to answer and was just making up answers. She didn't even know how old he was. She said he was three, and I yelled, "He's six! I've had him for six years." She got quiet. The employee just wrote down their notes and started talking about their programs and how they find new owners.

When I handed his leash over to the employee, I felt like my heart was being ripped out of my chest, like my true love was being completely broken at the hands of my own mother. Right then and there, I hated her. I felt no mother-daughter bond between us. I hated her for what she was making me do. My dog, my only protector for years, and she made me get rid of him the day after I get to New York.

When I was walking to the car, I could see Bruno through the door staring at me. He had never been without me his whole life until I went to my aunt and uncles after telling on my dad. I'd finally gotten him back just to give him to these strangers. I hated her. I hated her more than my dad at that moment.

On the way home, Mom was crying, begging for me not to hate her. She was telling me how sorry she was, pleading her case. She'd only had her dog for six or seven months. He was still a puppy and would have found a great home easier than my six-year-old Rottweiler mix that only loved me.

Once again I felt alone.

The first week of being there, she'd made me get rid of my dog. Then I realized she also told everybody why I was there. She told my brother, who turned around and told the whole freaking neighborhood. Anytime I went outside to play with the kids, I would forget everyone already knew, and they would bombard me with questions.

My mom also took me to her job, where I had complete strangers hugging me and telling me how sorry they were for me. I honestly regretted telling on my dad. Because of telling on my dad, I was sent to this place, where Mom had me get rid of my dog and where all her friends spoke to me like I was some patient. It was like I was a walking pity party, all because my mother couldn't keep her mouth shut. She was one of those people who liked to gossip about other people's hardships so she would get sympathy and attention.

A couple months went by, and I was still getting used to it all. I realized Mom never put my suitcase in the car like she said she would, so I had barely any clothes to work with while I was there. The Crisis Center had to pay for the shipping, which was like sixty dollars or something like that, so I went a couple months with just a couple outfits until Mom paid for it to be shipped.

My mom would work and leave me and my brother at the house. I stayed away from him as much as I could. He was still doing awful things to animals, like he used to do to my dog and my sister's cat. We were sitting on the couch, and my brother was like "Felicity look at this" and started laughing. He gathered as much spit and saliva as he could, opened Argus's mouth, and spit in it. I was so disgusted I almost threw up. But my brother just laughed and laughed like it was the funniest thing. He said he did it to him all the time.

Argus was quite aggressive. When Mom would feed him, you couldn't go near his bowl or walk past him without him growling and showing his teeth at you. He ended up snapping at my brother, which I didn't feel too bad about seeing how my brother treated him. He was just a dog that I didn't trust. He had a chemical imbalance or something. It got to a point where he was so aggressive that Mom decided to get rid of him.

So she made me get rid of my dog, that I'd had for six years and who was not aggressive toward anybody other than my dad, just to keep her puppy, and then she ended up getting rid of her puppy anyways. I was furious. That made me hate her even more. I called the Humane Society to see if my dog was still there. I would call over and over and over. I always got the same answer: "Sorry, once you release a dog into our care, we can't give you information on him. You would have to come see if he's on the floor for adoption."

For a couple weeks I begged Mom to take me, but she kept saying, "He's probably gone; he's probably gone." I begged her to go look for him. She finally took me, and he wasn't there. I felt a black hole where my heart should be. I started feeling hatred toward everyone, everything, even myself. I couldn't stop thinking about Bruno, hoping he was OK and in a safe home. I really wished that he didn't hate me, that he knew I loved him.

EIGHTEEN

After some time living with Mom and my brother, we moved to a town in upstate New York. It was a small town—you could probably drive from one side to the other in less than ten minutes. Our house was a five-minute walk away from the school. I liked it. Everyone seemed to know each other. Once I started school, I was able to meet new people. I made some really good friends that made me feel not so alone. I even had my first boyfriend.

Living with Mom was not going how I'd expected, that's for sure. It was more like a roommate situation and less like a mother-daughter situation. She worked a lot, so it was just my brother and I quite a bit. That didn't really last long though. My brother and Mom got into this huge fight. He left and walked all the way to Geneva. He ended up in some type of shelter. (That's actually where he met his ex-wife, the one that took his daughter away for a few years. She's a psycho.) Then it was just me at home a lot by myself.

I made friends pretty quickly. My boyfriend's sister and I became best friends, and it ended up being the four of us all the time—my boyfriend, his sister, and her boyfriend, which happened to be my boyfriend's best friend. We did everything together—sleepovers, parties, going to friends' houses, walking to school, all of it. We four were inseparable. None of them asked a lot of questions about my past, and I really liked it because none of them knew my situation. Therefore, they didn't feel pity for me and treat me differently.

I still had to live with my mom though, unfortunately. Anytime I asked for anything, she would say she didn't have the money. The only time she would really buy anything for me was on my birthday or at tax time. At tax time she would go all out and take me shopping, acting like she deserved the Mother-of-the-Year award. I don't remember ever having a serious in-depth conversation with her. Anytime I would speak and try to talk to her, she would cut me off and talk about something that had to do with her. My mom was just a selfish person, and I had to get used to that.

I was looking for something in my mom's room one day, and I found this paperwork with my name on it. I opened it up and realized it was my sister's and my statements the night I told on my dad. I was young; I didn't understand the system and how it worked. All I knew was that I was infuriated, knowing that my mother had read what we'd said. I thought it was none of her business. Then I got angry when I realized she'd seen what we said about Dad but still hadn't talked to me about it. She'd never said anything to me. All she'd ever said was that she was sorry and she hadn't known—that had been in the car on the way to New York—and that had been it.

I sat on her bed reading the statements. Tears were coming down my cheeks; I didn't realize that until my boyfriend came in and asked me what was wrong. I told him nothing, and he came over and wiped my face. He said, "Why are you crying then." At this point I hadn't told him anything; he had no idea. I felt this overwhelming feeling that I should tell him. I told him everything:

How my dad had molested me all my life. How I'd told on him, and now I was with my mom. I could see the sympathy growing in his eyes.

He looked down at the papers and said, "What's that?" I told him what it was, and he said, "Come on." He got up and walked and I followed.

He took me outside, in between my house and the neighbor's house. He said, "Give me the papers." I handed them to him, and he held them up and said, "You should burn them. Burn these papers and let go of your past. Don't let any of them hurt you anymore."

I grabbed the papers and the lighter and lit them on fire. I dropped them onto the ground, just watched the words burn and turn to ash. I felt liberated somehow. I felt lighter, like I'd set down the bricks that had been on my chest for so long, even if it was just for the moment. Right then and there, I decided I would not be a victim. I would not allow people to tear me down. I was going to be strong. I truly did feel better.

Mom got home later that day from work. I was on the couch with my close friends crying. I asked her why I'd never spoken to a judge or a lawyer. I asked her why nothing had ever happened after I told. She told me that the case was dropped because they didn't believe us; that Dad was in the military and well respected; that they believed what he'd told them. He told them we lied to go live with Mom because he was too strict. I was so hurt. Once again someone did not believe me when I'd finally found the courage to tell. I decided to not let it bother me. I shouldn't be angry no one believed me, because I had my friends who did believe me.

About a year went by: me always having arguments with my mom about her behavior and how she needed to act like a mom; her always working or going to the bar with her boyfriend or friends; me and my group, the four of us.

I don't remember how it happened. I don't remember if he

reached out first or if I did, but I started talking to my dad on the phone. He was always asking me if I was OK or if I needed anything. Months went by like this, talking to him randomly on the phone for a little while, giving an update on what I was doing and how I was doing.

I remember talking to my boyfriend's sister, my best friend at the time, and I told her I was thinking about visiting my dad, seeing how he was. She was shocked. She asked if I was sure I would want to do that. I told her he still had a power over me that I needed to take back, and I wanted to ask him why. Why did he do those things to me? I needed closure, fully, to move on. After speaking to her, I decided I was going to visit my dad. If he'd lived alone, I wouldn't have gone. I think I would have been too scared still, even though I was trying to be brave.

He had actually moved in with his ex-girlfriend and her new boyfriend and my sister. I guess my sister hadn't been following my aunt and uncle's rules and they'd kicked her out, so she'd moved in with Dad's ex-girlfriend. Kind of weird they all lived under one roof. Knowing his ex-girlfriend, who I really cared for, was there as well as my sister, I knew I would be safe if I visited him.

I arrived in Tennessee, and I hugged my dad. Like I said before, I loved him. Everything was weird though, like I could feel tension, like there was this huge pink elephant following us around. We got to the house, and I saw my sister and I hugged her. We both just cried. She showed me her room, and we lay on her bed talking for a little while before she went to work. I slept in her bed with her, where I felt most comfortable anyways. We talked about everything—life, boys, Mom, Dad—everything we could think of.

The second night, Dad and I were alone for a few hours in the evening; my sister was at work, and my dad's ex-girlfriend and her new boyfriend were out. Snickers, our family chocolate Lab, was lying down on the floor. I was sitting on this bench-like seat. My dad sat next to me and said he thought we should talk since we were alone. I instantly felt my chest get tight, and I got really nervous. I'd never once spoken to my dad about what he'd done to me. Never. I was really scared and nervous; I couldn't even talk.

He started by telling me that he was sorry for ever hurting me. He said that he didn't remember doing everything we said. He told me that he remembered doing some things to me but didn't remember ever touching my sister. He then said that he'd been heartbroken after my mom left, and I looked just like her.

I just sat there. I was almost sixteen; it had been almost two years since I'd lived with my dad, and here he was, on his knees crying. He was begging for my forgiveness. I couldn't fully take in anything he said or question any of it. All I could say was "I forgive you."

As I sit here, as an adult, I am so disgusted with his reasoning behind it all. I wish I had thought more clearly back then so I could question him. My dad saying he was heartbroken after my mom left—saying I looked just like her—it didn't make sense, because he used to leave his bed with his wife, my mother, in it to come to my room. My mother would be sleeping next to him, and he would feel the urge to come to my room and do what he did. The fact that he said he didn't remember touching my sister—he'd touched her first. She just woke up easier than me, so he stopped doing it to her earlier, and he kept doing it to me for years and years. Saying that he didn't remember what he'd done—such a cop-out. This, once again, showed how much of a coward he was. But like I said, I was a sacred sixteen-year-old. I didn't get the chance to say any of these things that I think about now as an adult.

After that night, the trip went well. I spent time with my sister and my dad. When the week was over, I was sent back to New York. My dad and I spoke frequently then. He even started sending me three hundred dollars a month to help toward things I needed that my mom wouldn't buy.

My dad actually came to visit a few months later. He stayed at Mom's house, with us on the couch. He even met my boyfriend, which terrified me. My boyfriend was half black and half Italian, and my dad was never OK with the idea of one of his daughters dating a black man. He actually said really nice things about my boyfriend after meeting him, which surprised the hell out of me. When I told my sister, she was shocked and pissed because Dad acted differently with her dating anybody that was a different race.

When Dad was there visiting, my mom acted as if they were together again. She wouldn't stop laughing, giggling, and flirting with him. Here I was, forgiving my dad for every bad thing he'd done to me, yet I was sitting there judging my mom because she was still not angry with him. She never had been. I guess I just couldn't understand it. Hell, I still can't.

NINETEEN

Being at Mom's, I felt like my life was going nowhere and would never go anywhere. I knew I didn't want to end up like her or end up like all the other people in that town. I had a great relationship with my first boyfriend, but as sad as it is to say, I didn't see him going anywhere in life. He didn't have anyone pushing him to do better either. His mom wasn't happy with her life, and his dad was in and out of prison. He had a lot of potential to do great things, but he just wasted it.

It should have been harder for me to leave, but it wasn't, and that's how I knew that I needed to go. I was with Mom for a couple of years, and I had a good boyfriend and a best friend, but that was it—that's all I had. It wasn't enough to make me stay. I was just about seventeen when I decided to move back in with my dad. I said goodbye to everyone, saying that I would see them again, but honestly, I wasn't too sure if I would.

Dad drove to New York, picked me up in the truck, and we headed to Tennessee. This felt different then all the times I was terrified to drive with him in the car. I felt like I was finally in control, and he knew it. I was no longer that scared little girl. It felt more like being with a roommate, kind of like how it felt when I first moved in with my mom.

He was living in this little apartment-condo type of place, and our dogs got along really well. He was in the process of buying a house so I could have my own room. I was able to do whatever I wanted—stay up as long as I wanted, leave and come back when I wanted. This was a huge change from when I'd last lived with him. He ended up buying a house in Tennessee.

The house was beautiful, probably the best house I ever lived in. My room had a lock on the door, and I could lock it whenever I wanted; he never said anything. I still did chores and cleaned up, but that was the only rule really, other than that I had to go to school or work. Dad took me to test for my GED. I took the practice test and passed it, so I didn't have to take the classes. About a month later, I took the final test and received my GED.

I decided not to go to college right away but, instead, to work; since I was only seventeen, I felt like I had time before I had to go to college. Dad went half in on a car for me so I could drive myself when I got a job. It was a little purplish-blue Mazda Protege—such a crappy used car but I loved it. That Mazda was mine, and I felt this sense of freedom that I'd never felt before.

I started working for an inventory company, and I would work crazy hours, sometimes 1 a.m. to 7 a.m. or 10 p.m. to 2 a.m. I would go to parties and hang out with friends. I would be out all night drinking and smoking cigarettes. Dad was a whole different person. He wasn't judgmental or mean. He let me do whatever I wanted. We never argued, and most importantly, he never invaded my sleep again.

I felt like he was scared of me, but he also wanted me in his life. He never tried anything inappropriate with me. He started becoming the dad that he should have been from the beginning. He actually seemed like he cared. After a while, Dad's friend Andrew moved in. They had one thing in common: they'd both dated Patricia. She was the one my sister moved in with after my aunt and uncle kicked her out; also the same person my dad ended up moving in with.

Andrew and Dad would drink all night, watching TV and talking shit to each other. I felt like I was going down the wrong path. I was drinking every night, showing up to work drunk, driving drunk. I remember one morning waking up at 10 a.m. after working all night. I could hear the ice machine, and I knew any time I heard that ice machine, Dad was making a drink—whiskey and Coke. I remember lying in my bed, hearing him make his drink in the kitchen, and thinking to myself, *What am I doing? I don't want to end up like him, like an alcoholic.*

A few months after being at the new house, new neighbors moved in across the street. They were a young couple. They were really nice and had the cutest dog. After a few weeks of getting to know them, I realized they were trying to have a baby. I thought about that one night—if they had a baby, I hoped it would be a boy so Dad wouldn't do anything.

The wife and I were chatting one night, and we ended up talking about our childhoods. She told me about the abuse she suffered growing up. I felt comfortable, so I told her about mine; about Dad. I even shared with her that I thought I was pregnant. We both cried, and I thought we were pretty close. Then she said that, if I was pregnant, would I give the baby to her; that I was too young to be a mother. The conversation got really weird after that. I just nicely said I had to go. She hugged me and I left.

A few months later, she asked me to house/dog-sit for her while they were on vacation. Of course I said yes, and I would go over there and stay the night so their dog wasn't alone, then I would let him out throughout the day. The last day, I walked over there, and her door was wide open. I was scared and went to get one of the neighbor boys that was older than me. He walked through the house with me, and we didn't see anyone. I called the police. Then I called her to tell her that I shut her door and someone had been in the house.

Well, a week or so after that I was at work, and the neighbors both came over and told Dad that they thought I'd stolen from her—a laptop and jewelry or something. They then asked my dad if they could search my room, and he allowed them. She picked up a shirt she had given me months before and told Dad that it was hers. Then they sat in the living room talking until I got home.

I came in—Dad had a drink in his hand, and the neighbor was sitting there with the shirt in her hand. She then started crying, telling me she'd trusted me and she couldn't believe I would steal from her. I told her I didn't and reminded her it was a shirt she had given me months before. She then yelled and said she was pressing charges. Then they left.

Dad said, "Well did you." I told him no of course not. He said, "Well, I don't know if you did, but she told me that you told her what I did to you all those years ago. Oh, and you might be pregnant!" I denied the pregnant part of it, but I told him I did tell her about what he did. He got so mad at me—yelled and screamed—saying if I couldn't let it go then I would have to leave. He wouldn't let me stay there with him if I still felt the need to bring it up. A week later he apologized for letting them in my room without me there and for not believing me. I chose to forgive, once again.

After about a year and a half of living with Dad, I decided to move back to New York. He was sad; he gave me a big hug and we said our goodbyes. I felt like we left on good terms; there was no hatred or ill will.

I got in the car with my dog, Juju, and started my trip back to New York. I stopped in Pennsylvania to see my *popou*—he was my mother's dad. I loved him to pieces. He had no idea what had happened with Dad or what he'd done, and I kind of wanted to keep it that way. He was such a sweet and loving man, and I didn't want to ruin anything for him. Ever since my *yiya* had died, his wife, I'd felt like I had to do whatever I could to make sure he was happy, and telling him about my dad definitely wouldn't have made him happy.

After driving to Pennsylvania and spending a couple days with my popou, I continued on my trip to New York. When I arrived, Mom was over-the-moon happy that I was back. She seemed different—more grown-up, I guess you could say. She lived in a trailer in Canandaigua. She was still working for the state, but she seemed happy. Her trailer had a college no more than a couple blocks away from her house, and I thought about going to it. I wasn't in any rush to go to school, so I took a little bit of time; I did what I wanted to do.

I had been back for a few months, and I would often go to this gas station down the street to buy cigarettes, because they accepted my Tennessee ID. At the gas station right next to us, the teller would never sell to me because of my out-of-state ID. This one time, I took Juju for a car ride to that gas station down the road, and there was this really cute guy outside smoking a Black and Mild. He saw Juju and asked if he could pet her. I told him, "Yeah, that's fine," and that's when he told me he had a pit bull too. I got so excited because I used to take my dog to the dog park in Tennessee, and she loved playing with the other dogs.

That's when I asked him if he would want to meet at a dog park or something. He was all for it, asked for my number, and I gave it to him. I left the gas station pretty excited that my dog was going to have a friend.

After a couple days, I decided to give him a call to let him know I was heading to the dog park. Awkwardly, he said, "Oh, I'm heading into class right now." He called me back later that night and we talked. That's when I realized he thought I was cute and had wanted my number, so he'd used my dog as a reason to talk to me.

I guess I owe his dog, Nina, and Juju a big thank you for giving my now husband an excuse to speak to me that first night we met.

TWENTY

After just a few days of talking, my husband and I pretty much lived together. I know that sounds crazy, and it definitely was, but we were happy. We were spending every second together. We honestly fit so perfectly, like yin and yang. He was so laid back and I was not; he was quiet and shy and I was not. We just meshed so well.

He was a student at the college that was down the road from my mom's house, and he had a dorm room off campus. I would go there every day and every night. I remember him sitting on the floor, leaning on the bed, and I was behind him on the bed with my arms wrapped around him. Something on the news came up about a man molesting his children, and I instantly became anxious. Then he said, "Anyone who does that deserves death."

This statement truly upset me. I felt so broken by his comment. I wasn't upset that he felt that way; it just upset me that it pertained to what happened to me in my life with my father. I instantly started thinking, *Great, I either never tell him and hope he never finds out, or I tell him and he's never OK with my father being in my life or meeting him.* I was torn.

Here I was, upset but unable to tell this man, who I was falling in love with, that my dad molested me for more than half my life. My mind was reeling, thinking, *What if we have kids? What if we don't because of this? What if he thinks I'm disgusting? What if he never wants my dad in my life? What if he doesn't understand? What if he doesn't want me in his life?* I was devastated.

I was so torn on whether or not I should ever tell him—if this should again be a secret that I kept to myself. I just felt like he would never understand, and he would never have an open mind to meeting my father or understanding why I allowed him back in my life. Either way, it all felt too difficult to deal with, so I ignored it. The problem with that was, because of the things my dad did to me, I wasn't able to do certain things with my husband most women would want to do with the man they're falling in love with.

A few weeks after that night, we were lying in bed, and he tried to kiss me again; he was trying to push his tongue into my mouth. I had been able to pull away or avoid it before, but this time he pulled at my pants and started kissing me down my body to my vagina. I grabbed him and told him no. I could see he was getting upset, like I was denying him. I ended up realizing that I had to tell him; he needed to know that it wasn't him. It was me.

I told him I needed to tell him something awful and that I wasn't sure how he would take it. I told him my dad molested me, and because of the things he did to me, there were certain things that I wasn't sure I would ever be able to do sexually. I asked him if he was OK with that, and of course, being the most perfect human being he is, he looked at me and said "I'm glad you told me, and I'm sorry for making you feel that way. I didn't know. I had no idea."

He asked me questions like any curious person would, and I kept my answers very short and nondescriptive. I shared just enough information for him to understand the severity of it all. He never pushed me to tell him, but he did ask me why I had let my dad back in my life. I told him that he was all I'd had for years—when my mom left, my dad was all I had. My husband asked me what would happen when I had kids of my own, and I told him my dad could be in their life, but he would never be left alone—ever—with any of my children. And he nodded like he understood.

I was terrified, thinking this could ruin what could be a beautiful relationship, a beautiful marriage; but when I told him, he made me feel better. He made me feel like I could talk to him about anything. It really solidified how much I loved him and how much he loved me. It showed how understanding and sweet he was. I remember thinking, *How did I get so lucky to have a man like this.*

After some time, my husband and I had a baby boy. I remember being pregnant, sitting on his bed in his dorm room, eating a Pepperidge Farm cake that was in the freezer aisle at the grocery store—three layer chocolate cake. We wouldn't even cut it up to put on plates; we would just sit in his bed, open the box, and eat it with two forks. My husband would always be there when I would wake up at two or three in the morning with a McDonald's craving. He never complained, not even once. He would just say, "Let's go," or "Do you want me to go get it for you?" I swear he went through the same cravings I did.

Nothing compared to the day that I had my son. Mom was actually there with me, supporting me for the first time. It was like she had changed completely for the good. She stayed with me the whole time. Mom was being so attentive and loving. She cried when she saw our son for the first time. I cried seeing her like that. We had an awful mother-daughter relationship throughout my whole life, but I knew, with the positive changes she had made over the years, she was going to be the perfect yiya. After some time of loving on her new grandson, Mom had to leave to get ready for work.

My husband had to go to work too and would be coming back

to the hospital after. I called him and said, "I am absolutely starving but they won't let me eat." He went and bought me McDonald's, which I loved at that time. He hid it in his backpack and smuggled it into the hospital for me. We sat on that hospital bed quickly eating together before the nurses came in and saw us.

A few hours after that, I had to go to the bathroom. When I came out, I saw him standing by my son just rubbing his hand on his cheek. I remember looking in my husband's face, and he had nothing but pure love and adoration for his new son. Tears started streaming down my face from pure happiness. How was I so lucky to have a man like him; to have a man that treated me with nothing but respect and love; a man that would be a wonderful father and a great husband one day. I really did hit the jackpot with this one guys.

TWENTY-ONE

After my son was about six months old, I decided I wanted to drive to Tennessee to see my dad. I wanted him to meet his grandson. I was nervous to talk to my husband about this because I knew how he felt about my dad and the whole situation. He was surprisingly understanding when it came to me wanting to visit my dad. My husband hugged me and told me that whatever I wanted to do, he would be there for me.

I spoke to my sister, who was married and with her first son at the time, and we decided to visit together. My husband, my son, and I packed up and headed to Tennessee. My sister, with her husband and son, met us there. In the end, there was no awkwardness between any of the men. I was really surprised, but I also knew how good my dad was at putting on an act—the master deceiver. Having us all there at the same time felt natural. There was no awkwardness; it seemed to go as it would with a normal father meeting the men in his daughters' lives for the first time.

My husband and I were talking in our room after the first night, and he said that it was crazy to know what my dad had done and to see how he was now. You would never have known that he was an abuser, because he put on a really good act as a normal person, father, and friend. I told him that my dad was a master at tricking people into believing he was a stand-up guy. He had been doing it his whole life. We did agree that my dad would never be alone with our children, ever, in any situation. My husband said that he would follow my lead and have my back in any decision I ever made

The trip went well. It was even fun—we laughed a lot. We did tourist stuff with my sister and her family. We drank a little and grilled, hung out with family and friends. Then we headed home. It went on like this for years: everyone getting along and no issues from my past coming to haunt me. Everything seemed fine.

My husband and I ended up having a daughter. She was our miracle baby. Dad came to visit a couple times, and those visits were also nice and what you would call normal. My life was great. It felt like I'd fixed my relationship with my dad. I had a great boyfriend and two beautiful children. Mom was a great yiya to my kids. Everything was good. I was happy. My soon-to-be husband and my dad got along. My dad was acting like a normal father and grandfather should. I even had him walk me down the aisle when my husband and I got married.

We all hardly argued. That is until a few days after the wedding. The day my dad was leaving after the wedding, we were at my mom's house saying our goodbyes. Dad was talking to Mom about my sister, saying she had always been in her own little world and that she had been lucky to have my aunt and uncle in her life for as long as she did. Then Dad said that she'd ruined her chances at a better life because she'd messed up there and got kicked out.

My dad's girlfriend looked at me and said, "I don't know how she could treat them like that. I love your aunt and uncle. They're the best people I've ever met."

I looked at her and said, "No, they're not."

My dad's girlfriend was a little taken aback, and she asked me, "What do you mean."

I said, "Nothing forget it." I gave my dad a hug, and they left.

About 2 a.m. that night, I got a text from my dad talking crap. He was mad that I said that about my aunt and uncle to his girlfriend. He said she was asking him questions now and asking why I would say that. He said he felt like I had said that on purpose to force him to talk to her about what had happened between us. Then he ended the text with "I don't want to live through that hell again."

I was so livid, I texted back, "What do you mean live through that hell again? Like you're not the one that caused it!!!" How dare he talk to me like that! How dare he blame me and try to silence me once again. I was so mad because of that argument, and I didn't talk to him for almost a year. I would have gone longer if he hadn't messaged me. He ended up telling me he was sorry and that he overreacted. Once again, he asked me to forgive him.

Like a fool I did.

I don't understand why I felt the need to have a relationship with him. After everything he'd done to me, everything he took from me, I still felt like I needed my dad in my life. To this day I don't understand why I felt that way. I would be sad when we would have to leave. We would talk almost every day about anything— life, kids, relationships—but I never could forget what he'd done. I would think about it all the time, about how he had been a monster then. My sister and I would even talk about it and cry still. Even with all of that, I felt like I needed my dad in my life. He was literally the only person we had for years.

My whole life I felt like something was missing, like a part of me was missing. I never understood what it was. I just didn't feel whole. I reacted to situations differently than most would, and I hid my emotions well. I still do. I know that hiding my emotions helped short term, but I never realized how bad it would affect me long term.

I mean, I know that what he did to me caused me not to be able to do physical or sexual things with my husband or any man before him. I was unable to be a hundred percent honest with my feelings and experiences. Even with all that, I still couldn't help but feel I'd made it out easier than some people like me; that some people that were abused their whole lives ended up in worse situations than I, like drugs, depression, or suicide. I know what I went through brought me to the darkest days of my life. It brought me to the edge—brought me to thoughts of suicide and of murdering him— but I still feel like I'd made out better than I should have. How did I deserve such a wonderful life when I allowed such horrible things to happen to me? Then I would remember that it wasn't my fault. It was his. I didn't deserve a life of misery. I deserved my happy life.

After that argument with my dad and going almost a year without speaking, I realized, when we finally started talking again, that I knew I actually didn't need him; but I needed to know why I was deciding to have him in my life rather than not. I knew that I had never fully worked out my issues with him, yet I was quick to forgive him.

At least that was the case, until the day I smelled his soap.

My brother had moved in with me and my family for a little while (we thought). He'd bought Irish Spring soap to use, and it was in the shower. I honestly hadn't thought about that soap—never bought it, never even smelled it, since leaving my dad's house after telling my mom about the abuse.

I took a shower and grabbed soap without looking, and it happen to be the Irish Spring soap. I put it on my loofah and started to wash my body with it. I smelled it and instantly felt nauseous. I jumped out of the shower and went straight to the toilet. It took me a half a second to realize that the smell was what I would smell on my dad every time he came into my room.

I felt sick and felt numb. I hadn't had an issue like this for years; I thought I was over it. I thought I was healed, I guess you could say. After that, I completely fell apart, sobbing naked on the floor over the toilet.

I called my brother into the living room once I got myself together, and I explained to him he could not ever bring that soap into my house again. I told him why, and my brother, who used to be a jerk, was understanding. He seemed to actually believe what I was saying about my dad. For the first time he acted as if I wasn't lying—he'd always called us liars. He apologized, which I never thought he would do, and then he cried. He told me that, if he'd known, he would have done something. I felt he was being genuine about his feelings. I think that was the only time me and my brother actually bonded over something.

I was hopeful that I wouldn't have any more issues now that my brother wasn't going to buy that soap anymore. Unfortunately, the Irish Spring soap in the shower was the first of many episodes to come.

TWENTY-TWO

After the soap incident, I thought I would be fine. But a few months after that I had my first night terror. I woke up in an extreme panic. My husband was shaking me, telling me to wake up. All I remember is hyperventilating and crying. I couldn't form the words to tell my husband what I'd just dreamed. It felt like hours had gone by before I could fully breathe on my own. My husband was rubbing my back, telling me everything was going to be OK. He said I was crying in my sleep so he'd started waking me up.

All I remember of the night terror was lying in bed and looking over at my husband, lying there with his back to me, then looking over to the door and seeing this big shadowy figure. However, I do vividly remember the feeling that I felt when my husband woke me up—absolute dread, panic, and terror. I truly felt like I had when my dad used to come into my room.

My husband went to work the next morning, and I went to sleep since I didn't have to be up for work for another couple of hours. I had the nightmare again. I was able to wake myself up, but I couldn't breathe still; it felt like someone was sitting on my chest, crushing me. I felt like I was going to die. Once I was able to get myself together a little bit, I decided to call my sister-in-law. I didn't want to worry my husband while he was at work, and I didn't want to be alone. I called and I told her what was happening. I asked her to come over.

Her and her husband, my brother-in-law, came, and she hugged me. It was exactly what I needed, and I just cried. She was trying to do whatever she could to make me feel better. He was trying to tell me about the verbal abuse he'd suffered from his dad, and how it made him a stronger person. They both were trying so hard to make me feel better, but I was still just so upset. I kept asking myself, *Why is this happening to me now? Years and years have gone by, so why am I just now having these night terrors?*

My husband came home early, and we all sat there talking about it for a little while. When they left, I lay in my husband's arms and cried until I finally went upstairs and went to sleep. I was racking my brain, trying to figure out what had changed. Why was I dreaming about this now? Why was it affecting me now? It had been fifteen years since my dad molested me. None of it made sense—until I remembered that soap, that damn Irish Spring soap, that made me sick to my stomach. The smell had brought me back to the time when my dad was coming into my room at night.

I had another night terror a few days after, and each time I had one it progressed. In the first one, I was in bed with my husband. I looked over and his back was to me, and then I looked at the door and saw a shadowy figure. Then the nightmare progressed to the shadowy figure moving toward me until it was on top of me in my bed. It was so heavy that I couldn't breathe; I couldn't move. I was paralyzed like I had been when I was a girl.

Then a week or so went by, and the nightmare came back. It was the same exact thing at first: I look over at my husband and his back is to me. I look over at the door to see the shadowy figure.

It starts walking toward me until it's on top of me, crushing me; every breath I have is harder and harder to take. Then I smell it—cigarettes and Irish Spring soap—and I feel like it is burning my nose with every breath.

I finally decided that I needed to cut my dad out of my life. I was just allowing this toxic person to be in my life and in my children's lives. I was thinking, *How can he be so stress-free, knowing what he did, while I'm here, years later, struggling to even sleep, waking up every night from a night terror, screaming and crying?* It wasn't fair; he should suffer for what he did. He shouldn't be happily living his life and be perfectly fine.

I decided to text him. I wrote, "I've been having night terrors. About you. So bad that I wake up in a panic, crying, can't breathe. Started ever since I smelled my brother's soap. Irish spring. Soap you used to use when I was little. I know you probably won't reply to this. You never do when it comes to what you did to us. But I needed you to know. You may have gotten over it, and to be honest I thought I was too. But I was obviously wrong. I'm going to see a therapist. I need to get you out of my head. Before it starts fucking my life up. I was crying so loud in my sleep last night, my husband heard me from downstairs. I wouldn't forgive myself if the kids heard me. It would scare them so much. But I just don't know what to do. How to make it stop. You have never been held accountable for what you did all those years. Apologizing to me when I was fifteen, saying you were sorry, but I just looked so much like Mom. You did it to me while Mom slept in your bed. You did everything to me physically except actual intercourse. And you act like you did nothing wrong. Even your apology was half-assed. I love you, Dad, as sick as that is. But you can't be in my life or the kids life. Ever. I know you don't care what I am going through right now because of you. But I needed to tell you. It's been fifteen years since you last touched me, and I'm still having nightmares about it. Either you are sick in the head thinking you did nothing wrong or what you did wasn't bad. But either way, you're wrong. You molested me for so many years. And never actually took responsibility and apologized. Now I'm twenty-nine, and it's haunting me still. You like to live as if you never did these awful things. But just know I remember all of it. From the very first time when I woke up and you were sucking my toes. To the last time where my panties were by my ankles and your dick was between my thighs. I fucking remember all of it. And I'm having these fucking night terrors and panic attacks, and I don't know how to make it fucking stop. It's not right that you're able to move on and I'm not. You should be the one suffering not me. You ruined my childhood, and now your fucking with me mentally. I hate that I love you. I wish so much I didn't."

I sent that text August 23, 2020, on my birthday. He replied, "Dear Felicity: This is devastating, to say the least. The finality of goodbye is most difficult. But, of course, your health is of utmost importance. You guys will always be in my heart and on my mind. Love you all!"

I was so upset by this, I regretted having him back in my life and in my children's lives. I hated him. He didn't even care about what he'd done to me. This was when I felt like the biggest fool. All his lies, saying that he was sorry. I felt like an idiot for believing that he was better and changed for the good. He really could care less about what he did to me or what it was doing to me still. That right there gave me the courage to cut him out of my life and be positive that it was the right decision

The night terrors were still waking me up, and waking my husband up, in the middle of the night. I feel like the last night terror was trying to tell me something though.

My husband woke me up, shaking me to get me awake, then hugging and holding me while I had a panic attack. I decided enough was enough—I needed to see a therapist. When I finally found one, I spoke to the therapist about the night terrors. She literally spoke about everything except for what had happened with my dad. She kept saying, "I don't feel like you talking about it and living it over again is going to help you." She told me to take deep breaths before bed and think of an animal that could protect me or a person that could protect me. If I thought of that before I went to bed, then that would hopefully place them in my dream. I tried it a few times, but it never worked.

She and I actually didn't get along well, so I stopped going. I was terrified though; I had been hoping I could get through this before our friends camping trip that we went on every year. The last thing I wanted to do was to have a night terror in a cabin full of people, including my children, and scaring everyone half to death. I was having these nightmares a couple times a week, if not every day. I felt like it was never going to end.

A few weeks before the camping trip, I had another night terror that progressed further than before. In this dream, I was lying in bed, my husband with his back to me, the shadowy figure at the door, walking toward me. The shadowy figure walked over and then was on top of me, weighing me down, crushing me. I smelled the soap and cigarettes. Then he disappeared.

In the dream, I got up because my husband wasn't in my bed anymore. My vision was clouded, like I was drunk (but I wasn't). I walked through this long dark hallway, and I saw a shiny doorknob. I tried to reach for it a few times but kept missing it because of my dizziness. Then I finally got it. I opened the door, and I walked through a stairwell and then a hallway, into a living room. I saw my husband lying down watching TV. I lay down next to him, and I just cried and cried. He kept asking me if I was OK. "What's the matter? What's the matter?" But I couldn't get the words out. I was stuck—like I'd been when I was a girl—unable to speak or form the words to explain what I was going through or what was happening.

In that night terror, I felt drunk or drugged. I couldn't see straight. I was seeing double, and the doorknob was so hard to open; I couldn't speak. It started making me think that maybe my dad had drugged me all those years, and that's why it took me so long to move or fully wake up. Unfortunately, I'll never know the truth because he will never admit it.

I was disappointed in myself: I should have known better. All those years of trying to please him and make him proud. He didn't give a damn about me, not truly. I still regret having him in my life and in my children's lives.

My daughter asked me about him a couple times. I told her he was not a good dad. I allowed him to try to be a better grandpa, but, in the end, I thought it was best for us not to see him anymore. She's too young to understand; so is my son. I'm not sure I ever want them to know the whole truth. That is one of the biggest reasons I wasn't sure if I wanted to publish this book.

One thing I am certain of is he will never be allowed in my life again. He will never be allowed to have that power over me or my mindset. I refuse to allow that toxic piece of crap back in my family's life. I will never make that mistake again. I hope he gets what he deserves. He's never truly been held accountable; he never did jail time, never got help for his illness. No one believed my sister or myself. They just believed we wanted out of the strict household of a decorated Marine so we could go live with our mother. The funny thing was that my sister never even lived with my mom.

He always got people to believe him. They believed he was this upstanding guy. He was a master at deceiving people—he still is. You would never know that this gentleman, this Marine, this upstanding guy, was molesting his daughters while they slept. He fooled everybody, and he still does.

TWENTY-THREE

November 27, 2021, I had a night terror again. I hadn't had one in months. I was lying in bed; my husband was holding me, and he was asleep. We were in our yurt tent. In the dream, I opened my eyes and saw the shadowy figure of a man outside my tent by my bed. Then I heard my kids screaming for help at the tent entrance. (I realized it was a dream, but if you have kids, you understand the feeling that washed over my whole body.) I started panicking, trying to move. I couldn't. I looked over and saw my husband sleeping with his arm around me still. I start trying to scream, but it was like my mouth was glued shut. My kids were still screaming, begging for me to help them. I was paralyzed once again. I kept trying to scream, "Wake up! Wake up! It's just a dream! *Wake up!*"

Finally my husband woke me up. I was trembling, crying, hardly able to breathe. He rubbed my back and held me, telling me, "It's OK. It was just a dream, baby. You're OK; you're OK." After some time, I finally calmed down enough to ask him if he'd heard me. He said, "Yes, you were whimpering in your sleep." I started crying more and told him some of what the night terror was about.

He assured me nothing would ever happen to us again and that he would always be there to protect us.

I calmed down enough to lie back down, but I had this overwhelming feeling I should go in the house and check on the kids. I got up and said I had to check on them. My husband said that he would, and I just told him no, I needed to.

I got up and put my shoes on. I ran up the stairs and opened my son's door. He was awake, and I hugged him so tight. He asked me if I was OK. I said, "Yeah, I just had a bad dream and had to check on you."

He hugged me tight, telling me, "Ah, Mom, it's OK. I'm OK. I love you."

I went into my daughter's room; she woke up as soon as I opened the door. I went to her and hugged and kissed her. She said, "Mommy, are you OK?" I told her I'd had a bad dream and wanted to check on her and her brother. She hugged me so tight and kissed me, telling me everything was OK. She told me she loved me so much.

After I said goodnight to them, I went back to the tent and lay down with my husband. He held me tight, and I cried a little more, explaining the night terror more now that I was calmer. I told him I thought I'd had it because I'd just finished writing about it in this book. He said, "Baby, no more writing at night," and I agreed because I knew he was right. After he said that, we both went back to sleep.

Here it is, the next morning, and I am writing this. I needed to get it written down while it was still fresh. This is hard. I am crying as I type. I felt it was important to get it out.

When I say my father will no longer have power over me, I don't mean the night terrors will stop or that I will become a normal, fully functioning wife physically, or that I won't be over protective of my children due to what I went through. I mean he won't have power over me by keeping me silenced, by making me feel paralyzed. The hurt is done; the pain is done; I can't change what he has done to me. I can just do my best as a person, as a mother, and as a wife. I can do my best to get my story out there. To let my father know I will not be silenced. I hope it helps others find the courage to also speak up, get help, and not be silenced by their abuser.

LETTER TO MY DAD

December 16, 2021
Dear Dad,

I know you are mad, and I know you hate me now for writing this book and telling the world about the awful things you did. I just couldn't do it anymore. Almost my entire life, I have acted as if I was OK, as if I wasn't fazed. The day I physically got sick after smelling that Irish Spring soap and the night terrors started, I realized I was not OK.

Most people will not understand why I ever let you back into my life, and that's OK. I hate saying this, but I do love you. You are my dad. You were the only person we had for years. Your opinion used to matter so much to me, and honestly, if you had admitted you were wrong and tried to get mental help for your sickness, then who knows where our relationship could've gone. But you didn't.

You hide. You hide your true self from the world and have the audacity to call us liars. You know what you did to me all those years. You know the pain you have caused me and still are causing me. Ever since the day I got that text where you said "I don't want to live through that hell again," I knew right then and there I'd made a mistake. I should've never allowed you back into my life. You don't deserve to be in my or my family's life.

I hate that I love you. I wish more than anything that I didn't care about you. I hope this book helps others like me to speak up against their abusers like I am speaking up about mine, about you.

I had another night terror again last night. My husband woke me up and saved me from the hell I live in inside my mind, that mental jail you forced me into. I woke up to him hugging me, telling me I am safe. I cried in his arms, trying to breathe. When I finally calmed down, I got up to go to the bathroom, and as soon as I got to the entrance of the tent, I had a panic attack just with the thought of going outside. My husband was there to walk me into the house— to make me feel safe—something you never did. My husband cried holding me, feeling helpless. My night terrors not only hurt me, but now they hurt my husband. We cried together, and then he held me the entire night.

You hurt me every chance you got, over and over. My father, who was supposed to protect me from evil, ended up being the evil—the monster who invaded my room every night. I am not sure I will ever forgive you. And I will never forget. No matter where I end up when it comes to my feelings for you, I will never allow you into my life again. I will do whatever I can to keep the poison you are away from my children.

My children are being raised by loving parents who actually protect them from harm. My daughter will grow up knowing what it is like to have a loving and protective father. My son will grow up with a father who teaches him and doesn't harm him; who loves him and doesn't belittle him. My son and daughter will grow up feeling love and adoration from their mother. My children will never feel the pain you caused us, the torture you put us through.

You are nothing. You're an actor. An actor who puts on a show every day and night for his audience. I hope you seek help—not for me, but for yourself. You are a danger to this world. You are toxic waste that does nothing but poison the people around you. I am done letting you poison me. I will not be silent anymore. You don't deserve that decency.

This is goodbye. When you are on your deathbed, don't call me.

Your Daughter,
Felicity Allen

In daylight you hid your face
Masquerading as our father
Giving us a false sense of protection
Making us love you, making everyone love you
Pretending to be what we wanted so badly for you to be

At night you revealed yourself
Our own personal boogyman
Creeping after dark
Trying to hide within the shadows
But we closed our eyes to not see you
This can not really be you

Too afraid to speak the nightmares and our fears
We let our truth become silent
You hid yourself so well we would forget who you really were
Feeding our hearts with guilt and confusion

Years later, we open our eyes
We weep and mourn this man, our
father, who did not ever exist
We see you clearly for what you are now
The man who hides in the shadows
And now everyone will see you too

—Kristina Burdett